T0159571

How to Survive a Bullet to the Heart

How to Survive a Bullet to the HEART

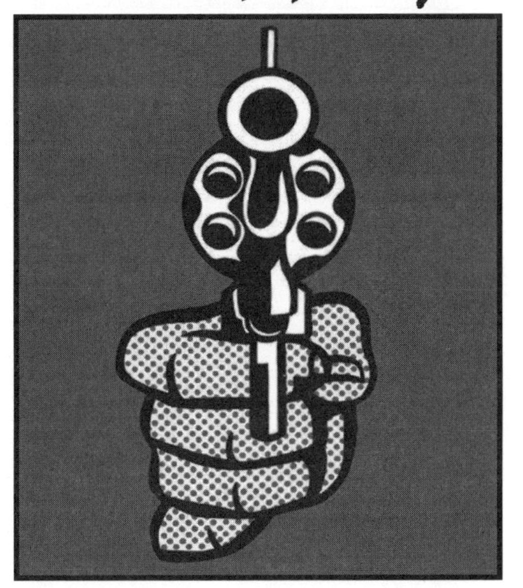

Secret Lives & Uncensored Confessions of Maximum Security Prison Inmates

Compiled, edited, and illumined by

JOHN WAREHAM

Such is the remorseless progression
of human society, shedding lives and
souls as it goes on its way. It is an
ocean into which men sink
who have been cast out by the law
and consigned, with help most
cruelly withheld, to moral death.
The sea is the pitiless social darkness
into which the penal system casts
those it has condemned,
an unfathomable waste of misery.
The human soul, lost in those
depths, may become a corpse.
Who shall revive it?
—Victor Hugo

HOW TO SURVIVE A BULLET TO THE HEART

WELCOME RAIN PUBLISHERS, LLC

ISBN 978-1-56649-399-4

COPYRIGHT © 2014
JOHN WAREHAM

THE EAGLES FOUNDATION
OF AMERICA, INC
www.eaglesgather.com

A NOT-FOR-PROFIT WHOSE MISSION IS TO
DEVELOP LEADERSHIP POTENTIALITIES FROM AND AMONG
THE OFFENDER AND EX-OFFENDER POPULATION.

PRINTED BY MAPLE PRESS
FIRST EDITION 2014

ALL RIGHTS RESERVED

ENQUIRIES TO
THE FLATIRON LITERARY AGENCY
flatironagency@earthlink.net

SALUTATIONS TO

DOWNSTATE TEAM
SUPERINTENDENT ADA PEREZ,
JUANITA CARMICHAEL,
MARVIN GALLAWAY & NEVILLE WELLS
and all who helped, especially the men
who so freely shared their inner journeys.

PAUL BLACKMAN, VAUGHAN EMSLEY,
RICHARD HABERSHAM, VICTOR HERLINSKY,
HEATHER MCRAY, TIMOTHY DEWERFF,
BRIAN O'DEA, JESS MAGHAN, BERNARD MINDICH,
SUSAN QUACKENBUSH, CRAIG RUBANO,
LOUISE WAREHAM, MARGARET WAREHAM,
JONATHAN WAREHAM, JOHN WEBER.

THE DEDICATED CLIENTS
whose support of my corporate leadership
development work, makes it possible for me to
serve pro bono in correctional facilities.

AND ALSO TO

Poets&Writers
&
State of the Arts

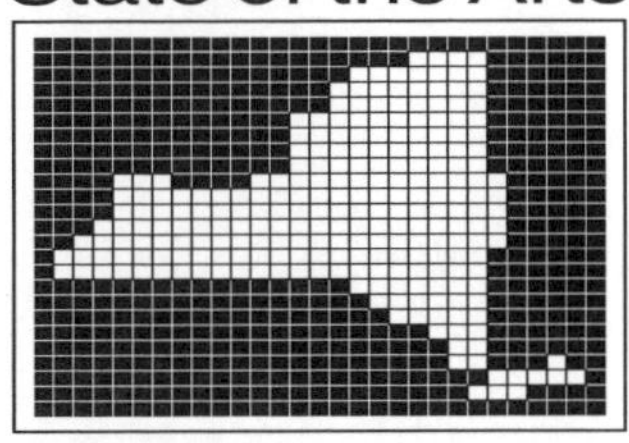

FOR THEIR GENEROUS SUPPORT

John Wareham, editor of this anthology, created the Eagles Foundation in 1996. An unpaid volunteer, he regularly presents the Taking Wings program in New York correctional facilities. Participants have consistently rated the Eagles program "best presented and most helpful." The low recidivism rate is unrivaled.

John's pro bono work is funded by his human resource practice, selecting and developing corporate leaders. A frequent keynote speaker, he was ranked by the *Financial Times* as "the hands down winner" among business communicators.

He has published several business best sellers in a dozen languages, including *Secrets of a Corporate Headhunter*, *The Anatomy of a Great Executive,* and the crossover life-changer, *How to Break Out of Prison.* A member of writers group PEN, his fiction includes the critically acclaimed *Chancey On Top*, and the national best seller, *The President's Therapist.* His *Sonnets for Sinners* was America's bestselling anthology of sonnets upon release on Valentine's Day 2010.

Dedicated to

—and inspired by—

the ideals and poetry of

Founding Eagle

Kenneth Johnson

(1953—2003)

and

the wisdom and perseverance

of Founding Eagle

Joseph T. Roberts

(1954—2007)

How to Survive a Bullet to the Heart

Contents

6. Doing the Time

7. Parole Hearings

Part Two

Surviving the Bullet & Breaking Free

8. Snakebite

What Got This Going

John Wareham

I've spent a lifetime advising corporations how to select and develop winning teams and leaders. One day an aspiring executive client with a drug habit wound up in Rikers Island, and gravitated to a rehab program.

Noting that I had visited him a few times, a program official asked if I might come along one day as a guest speaker. The class went well and I got asked back the next week–and then again, and again. That was nearly twenty years ago. I was–and still am–an unpaid volunteer so I enjoy the luxury of creating my own syllabus.

My clients include celebrated chief executives and I have always maintained a database of the psych-testing my firm created and routinely administers. I've personally known just about every senior executive who passed through my doors and typically get to see how my predictions pan out.

I subsequently expanded that database to include offender profiles. The wider, deeper window into human nature was enlightening. Working with violent offenders* in maximum security settings also sharpened my corporate coaching skills. I came to possess insights that others do not, which is just as well since that's how I earn my living.

This year, figuring it would be cathartic–and fun–I set the writing of a weekly poem as part of my prison class. Those poems–both rhyming and prose–were insightful and enriching. I think you'll be struck, as I was, by their honesty and wit, and the emotional journey's they reveal. As far as this genre goes, this is as good as it gets. I'm proud to share it with you. I have a lead-in to each of the sections, and, finally, an illumination of precisely what it takes to survive a bullet to the heart, so I hope you like those, too.

* Who, with very rare exceptions, were smart, courteous, and caring.

PART ONE

Crime & Punishment,
& Other Bullets to the Heart

The thing a lot of people cannot comprehend
is that Mother Nature doesn't have a bullet
with your name on it, she has millions of bullets
inscribed "to whom it may concern."
–Anonymous

We enter the battle for survival with the life we have, not the life we wish we had. So stuff happens. Then, fortunately, or so it seems, an opportunity to make things better presents itself. But as we attempt to seize the day the fates betray us. Our best-laid plans go awfully awry. In the twinkling of a diamond earring in a drug dealer's lobe, in the flicker of a dilated pupil, in the shudder of a pounding heart, in the twitch of a nervous digit, hapless souls become irrevocably intertwined and altered. The world turns and a mysterious journey begins.

1. The Moment of My Crime

Behind every great fortune lies a great crime.
–Honoré de Balzac

Hey, hang on a minute, Mr. Balzac. You're talking about robber barons from the past. Modern corporate officers mostly do the right and decent thing. Well, yes, okay, bad guys still make out like bandits. And, yes, our newest breed of dollar-driven attorneys, accountants, and auditors–and politicians–operate in an environment where it ain't a crime if you don't get caught. So, yes, white collar criminals mostly remain invisible. And, yes, even when they do get caught they mostly seem like upstanding citizens so almost never get to see inside a real jail. What we can wholeheartedly agree on, I think, is that as in days of yore, offenders who fail to make the cut are mostly from ghetto communities with single-parent homes and substandard schools ill-equipped to offer authentic education. Those schools can be dangerous places to enter–and especially to hang out in after hours. So, what to do? What if you're a young dropout who'd like to earn some of the moolah and attention so lauded by advertising and celebrity shows? Or what if you're the same young man who'd merely like to maintain a modicum of dignity and survive? What do you do–really? To quell your anxiety you could take a little something, a drink, a little weed, maybe even something stronger. Or, if you'd rather not topple into that poisoned well, you could take a course in the streets. It's free, and the heroes among your new friends–the guys with the gold chains, leather jackets, and Nike sneakers–will provide all the skills and training you need. Sure, there may be a little risk. But, hey, that's *business*–right? And, a man's gotta do what a man's gotta do to walk tall and put a little bread on the table.

Questions

Sheldon Arnold

Who am I?
What have I done?
I can't believe I did that.
What have I become?
Why are those guys oozing red?
That one looks just like he's dead.
They're staring at me, everyone.
Wherever did I get this gun?

Trumps

William King

I had to've been out of my mind.
Everything happened in slow motion.
My brain was skating on slime.
High as the moon, deep as the ocean.
I rolled with the earth but felt nothing.
The goal was merely to reprimand,
instead Death played trumps
with a ghastly hand.
Could neither sleep nor love
nor count the time.
Next day you could see in my eye,
that moment of my crime.

Incisions

Herburtho Benjamin

It is no gentlemanly jubilee,
incisions to prison play frantically;
I qualm to the cries of a banshee,
it cannot be, apparently,
yet further on it will be
a warning, ever, to me.
Shots blow by so rapidly,
what a travesty—a casualty hunting me;
this was surely never meant to be.
Still, I replied.

Moments

Ron Godbold

In that moment of my crime,
gratification filled my mind.
Lust entered my heart.
Greed tore me apart.
In that
single moment,
I lost my mind
and now
in every moment
I serve the time.

Wager

Joseph Birch

Common sense was my guide
or so I bet.
But the trap that naturally set,
I failed to heed—I'm no Jet!
If only I'd taken a moment to read,
but I failed in that
and now I fret....

Lost Sight

Neville Wells

Drunk on lye, driven by blight.
Blinding light—lost sight.
A hurtling dagger in the night.

The brain is bloating,
drifting, floating, sugar coating;
car goes sailing, ends on railing;
sirens wailing, life is trailing.

Shoulda Knew

Rudy Bisnauth

Summer's night, air blew,
quiet, somehow true.
Untold faces, cold stares,
reluctant glares,
stick to you like glue.
Temperamental escalator,
up and down,
run or freeze
which ride is true?
In the moment of my crime
I swear I shoulda knew.

Déjà vu

Moises Colon

Four and a half years but out now!
It feels damn good to ride a subway train.
For ten sweet weeks I feel so proud.
and then—Oh, No! Cuffed again.

Shackled to my partner in criminal descent
we fall upon the road,
our noses to pavement.
His eyes seek mine and his lips pucker
Mo, Mo, it's déjà vu, and oh so queer:
Last night I dreamed, and felt this fear,
and now, again, it's me and you, right here!
You shoulda told me motherfucker.

Infinity

Andre Rivera

My wounds are foul and petrify
because of my idiotic strife.
And now I see, as through a glass darkly,
that just two things are infinite in life;
the universe and human stupidity.
But of the former there's no certainty.

2. The Moment of My Arrest

Anticipating his own ultimate arrest by that hooded fellow with the wicked scythe, William Shakespeare comforted his dark lover, saying, *But be contented, when that fell arrest / without all bail shall carry me away / my life hath in this line some interest / which for memorial still with thee shall stay.* In the unforeseen, abrupt, up-ending moment of his own arrest, every one of our prison poets knew he'd be facing serious time; that he'd be torn from his loved ones and might indeed die in jail. Their racing thoughts and pounding feelings are therefore of particular interest–and for memorial still with thee shall stay.

Mother's Advice

Josue "Big Bear" Pierre

In the moment of my arrest.
I confess I was depressed,
and that mother knew best.
Son lay down and rest your feet.
Why roam the street like a dog in heat?
But mom, how'm I gonna eat?
I gotta get out and hustle the street.
Sow the wind and reap the gale
You'll end up like the rest,
dead and bleeding in an alley
or rotting in jail
and for all for what–a quick sale?
I promise, one day,
I'll put all this to rest,
meantime I'll be safe
in my bulletproof vest.

See now, Josue,
you've landed in jail!
It must feel like hell,
alone in your cell.

But I'm at peace;
you're alive and well;
better that than you
died in the street
to make a quick sale.

You created this mess,
use the time for the best.

Life's just a test,
and mother knows best.

Cold Entry

Richard Moore

In the moment of my arrest
I was embarrassed and ashamed,
So I tried to point the finger,
needed someone else to blame.

Had to find my true self
            and an honest friend
            for truth to unfold.
It's a lonely world with no one to trust
            and also very cold.

Initial Test

Joseph Birch

It was my initial test.
The removal from my shoulder
    of a chip.
The knot went out of my chest
in the moment of my arrest.

In jail you don't brush your teeth
    with Aim, Colgate, or Crest.

In the moment of my arrest,
I held my breath, it felt like death.
I did my best to stay strong,
    for all my wrong.
For how long do I sing this song?

New York Journey

Herburtho Benjamin

Screeching from downtown
wheels grind the ground,
the world's upside down,
no smiles just frowns.

A flying barrow
jammed with sorrow
no tomorrow
what will follow?

Shackles rattle,
potholes battle,
bodies follow,
chest is hollow.

Carried away, carried away,
carted off to messy hassles,
lawyers fees and commissary,
dialing home for love and money.
For sure, it is no longer sunny.

That Moment

Neville Wells

Shrieking, banging,
  bullpen doors
swinging, slamming
  sweaty pores.
Howling, wailing
  piercing screams.
Failing of the bright,
  bright beams.
Empty eyes, sewer smells,
  slimy floors, vomit hells,
suffocating
  tear-drenched shame.
Who to blame?
  From womb to tomb.
  Oh God, Oh God, please save me.

The Bright Side

Moises Colon

A zillion images flash:
mother, daughter, school, career
–the good life gone in the twitch of an ear.

I was eating a steak with a comely wench;
now it's old bologna

and a cold steel bench.

A familiar journey opens near.
I'll not see the streets for years.
I cringe at what I fear.

Countless treks to court and back,
all ending in sad blind track.

The banality of prison life,
cardboard meals and moral strife.

But look upon the bright side, please.
If it's a test of the spirit
I'm on my knees.

Greetings

Andre Rivera

As a kid my weird thoughts
I always expressed.
No matter the obstacle
I did my best.
My laugh was cool, but in my heart
there was anxiousness.
I lived in the East,
'til my life went West,
and led to the moment
of my arrest.
We were surrounded by cops
but I could care less;
I was not, I believed
a person of interest.

He asked for I.D. but before
I got to no or yes
he came in with force
that seemed outright excess.
Hey, my freedom turned
on that unfair contest!
My rights I instantly
sought to protest.

I sat in the precinct
to be processed.
How will I ever
get out of this mess?
My phone call's a damnable
source of distress,
nobody's home,
back there in my nest.

I call every five minutes,
completely obsessed.
I was doing just great,
but still failing life's test.

My attorney sings sweetly
but the beak's unimpressed;
the conversation's akin
to nonsexual incest.
My inner frustrations
are hard to suppress;
these cops and the law
I begin to detest.
As I hear the verdict
my chest congests;
the sentence delivered
I'd never've guessed.
I'm shocked for sure
by the court's largesse;
Hey, God, if you're there,
did you acquiesce?

Well, yes! I got off in the past with sins
that no priest would confess
and so when I pass,
and they put me to rest,
and my soul leaves the flesh
and I face the last test,
I'll tell all my sins
and not try to impress,
and God will forgive me,
more or less,
and the Devil won't greet me
in hell as a guest.

Failure

Sheldon Arnold

Awake!
Flashlights and guns,
heart like a drum,
where there was light,
darkness comes.
I dare you to run
Words from a tongue
You'll be shot like a dog,
left fit for the morgue.
Handcuffed wrath,
Loss of breath,
pang-filled chest.

Do not fight
    and do not flail.
Ride the rocky
    road to jail.

Okay, so I failed!
    But then I learned,
    and altered
    my behavior.
And now I know that once to fail
    is not to be
    a lifetime failure.

Winged Bird

William King

Tight air, can't breath, weak knees.
A big winged bird above my head,
croaking like a vulture for the dead.
Am I asleep or dreaming?
Won't someone wake me please
Wake me now, wake me with a smack.
No–I know I am awake
for now my wrists are prisoners
bound tight behind my back.

The door clangs shut.
Stripes before my face
Chrome beneath my butt.

Whatever happened?
Someone die?
Someone lose a life?
Whatever it may be my friend,
it cannot be right.
My mom? I am an only child,
however will she live?
Yeah, says my inner voice,
and what about your kids?
If you never believed in God before,
now's the time to start.

On my knees, I seek forgiveness,
and the changing of my heart.
I come to you suffused with stress.
I know that I've not been the best,
but now I seek your mercy
in this moment of arrest.

3. Judgment Day

When I was a kid I used to pray every night
for a new bicycle. Then I realized
that the Lord doesn't work that way
so I stole one and asked Him to forgive me.
—Emo Philips

Only by coming face to face with a sentencing judge can we fully comprehend the meaning of the word "mercy." Those who seek it typically realize that they took their chances and failed. They fear the judge will say, "You suspended judgment, so now I'm going to bring it down upon you." Family members sitting in the courtroom—typically only a tearful mother and a distraught wife—dread the worst but hope for the best. Happily, the best judges make allowances for human frailty. They tend to agree with Roman consul Decimus Magnus Ausonius who two thousand years ago noted, "It is odious for a strictly abstemious reader to sit in judgement on a tipsy poet." They know that justice springs from sincere intuition of the soul, angry or gentle; that anger is just, and pity is just, and that cold, calculating judgment never can be, since even the wisest judge cannot pretend to accurately calibrate the human heart.

Manhood

William King

The elevator departs the basement
and shudders to the twelfth floor,
I see no window or casement
as they march me down the corridor.
Wooden hands open to let me in;
a mouth inside recites my sins.
My lover sits behind me weeping;
I turn and show a fearless grieving.
The judge's words are pruning shears,
You are hereby sentenced–eighteen years.
I become a tin man without tears.

Dished

Joseph Birch

All I could do was wonder why.
Nobody there was my ally.
I stood there with both hands tied,
a bird to be dished and fried.
The judge's face was a frozen pie;
as she pierced my heart with a beady eye,
I felt like a fly about to die.
I knew then I would join the flock,
doing time around the clock.
Time is the ticker
and now I'm the tock.

My Defence

David Hutchings

Hey man, I did not commit this crime.
This lady said you robbed her.
Hey man, she's lyin'.
She picked you out of a lineup.
Yo, the bitch is blind–
I look nothing like this cat;
he's a five-foot-five Hispanic,
and I'm six feet tall and black
–can't you see she got it wrong?
You all say that, and we've heard it too long.
It's time to stop singing that same old song.

The Judge Struck

Neville Wells

Darkness from light,
chest too tight.
Judge struck with might.
Head wants to fight.
When will it turn bright?

Repentance

Moises Colon

Cold steel shackles, courtrooms grand,
a scroll of charges and here I stand,
as a callous D.A. plays a deadly hand.
The judge's tongue, an icy knife
cuts my ears and my heart–*eighteen to life*.
The walls close in like a sandwich board;
the world turns as black as a gallows bird.
Was I psychotic or merely wired?
In the moment of my sentence
I said, fuck repentance.

Frames

Ron Godbold

I knew my life would burst aflame,
that things would never be the same,
that I could never shift the blame.
Was this the price for fame?
I should have stayed
inside my window frame.

Souls and Flesh

Sheldon Arnold

Fear-filled eyes,
heart full of rage,
feel like I'm blind,
my mind lost in a maze.
Guilty verdict! Huh?
Guess it's off to the grave.
At least I can work out, and start on my waive.
In the moment of sentence,
shortness of breath,
and gone was the soul
once part of my flesh.
Hard to suppress,
this pain in my chest yet
sixteen years was all she suggested.

Loved Ones

Andre Rivera

Loved ones and friends stand there
aloof from my plague.
My iniquities, burdens too heavy
for me to carry,
pass over my head.

When I looked back, all I saw
was swinging doors.
Then I found myself alone
within the room,
and contemplating
my detour.

Priorities

David Hutchings

In the moment of my sentence
I showed no repentance.
"I'm innocent of this crime."
The judge paid no mind.

My lawyer asked for the minimum,
the D.A. sought the max: "Give him sixty-five
—he'll never see the streets alive."
"Rather too much, but I'll make it close;
—I sentence you to thirty-two,
with five years post."

Goodbye New York City,
won't see you for a while.
Man I miss my city,
like a mother misses her child.

But I'll be back some day
and we'll hang out, okay?
Just me and you my friend,
a double play.

I really don't want to go but I have no choice.
I miss you already, you can hear it in my voice.

So it's goodbye New York City
—but until we reunite
I'll be with you,
in my dreams each night.

Treasure

Rudy Bisnauth

This must not be happening,
but maybe it is.
Center of attention?
Center of evil?
Call it what you will–I'm in!
What are we waiting for–my keen mind?
No, don't go there
my perspective is slime.

This must be a dream.
Am I walking in my sleep?
Why is everyone staring?
And why can't I think?

Boom!

The judge calls a number,
I hear gasps in the room.
Where are my feelings?
Not within this costume.

I was young that day,
was it long ago?
No matter
right now I'm solo
and ready to go.

The moment of my sentence,
in which I grew old
was a blessing
that led to repentance.
I will treasure it like gold.

4. My Ride to Jail

Come, let's away to prison:
We two alone will sing like birds in the cage:
When thou dost ask me blessing, I'll kneel down,
and ask of thee forgiveness: so we'll live,
and pray, and sing, and tell old tales, and laugh
at gilded butterflies, and hear poor rogues
talk of court news; and we'll talk with them too:
Who loses and who wins; who's in, who's out;
and take upon's the mystery of things,
as if we were God's spies....
–King Lear, Act 5, Scene 3

The core attraction of a cruise line vacation is that we can peacefully recline in a deck chair or loll around in a swimming pool enjoying a deep sense of purpose because a sage, silver-headed captain is ensconced on the poop deck, and the boat itself is speeding us towards a heavenly destination. For the convicted inmate, the ride to jail is both similar and different. The pilot of the Paddy Wagon all too often turns out to be a highly testosteroned young fellow with dreams of becoming a racing car driver. Lights flashing, and hitting both siren and accelerator at every red light, he gleefully hurtles through the night, oblivious to the panic suffered by his ill-starred cargo of handcuffed passengers, who toss like rag dolls in their windowless cabin as the wheels beneath them screech around every corner and shudder over every pothole. Such a ride delivers the sense of an irreversible transition along with the feeling that life really is going somewhere. There is also the heightened sense of vitality that springs from feelings of dread for the approaching hellish destination, and the hapless denizens thereof.

Fares

Neville Wells

Eye without tear,
numb with fear.
People leer,
          often jeer.
Shame too near.
Blame the beer.
He's no seer.

Socked the maxi
ride Death's taxi.
Siren blares
animal ensnared.

Locked up now,
beyond all doubt,
they will never
          let me out.
No one cares
for my despairs
I must pay
          Death's fulsome fare.

Detainee Rights

Rudy Bisnauth

A ride to jail
is the same as a hot ride to hell.
Blaring lights,
a sweaty night,
a hundred on the dash,
racing through traffic,
  Oh, Christ, we could crash
while snaking the white line
          on the LIE.
Hey, Officer can we turn on the A.C.?
You get no privileges–you're a detainee.

Dolls

William King

Gazing out the window
  as the billboards race,
thinking of the time I face.
Palms all sweaty in a hot tin bowl,
the wagon shakes, rattles, and rolls,
and we're fixed to a plank
          like raggedy dolls.
This bridge's thin,
  it's like walking a plank,
water on both sides
  and stinks, it is rank.
Chained to a fellow
  who looks most unwell
Will he throw up before
  I get to my cell?

Riding to Jail

Joseph Birch

First things first:
I failed.

Riding to jail.
  I'm a tail.

Riding to jail.
  It was not in the plan
  yet here I am,
  shackled to another man,
  trembling like a junket flan.

Riding to jail.
  Where will I land?
  Begging for a helping hand?
  Washing pots, scrubbing pans?

Riding to jail.
  Do I clear my head?
  Do I remain a tail?

Riding to jail.
  I went from dining fresh,
  to eating stale.

Feelings

Sheldon Arnold

Claustrophobic fears.
Oxygen's scarce.
Stomach's nauseous,
don't think I can hold
the swill in my guts.

Handcuffed too tight,
bound up without glory,
shoulda put up a fight,
gotta think of my story.

Can I escape?
It's now or never.
Okay, then–never.
It was a short ride to jail,
but it felt like forever.

Trussed on the Bus

David Hutchings

There's no peace, no justice; the system's unjust.
It's just us, handcuffed on buses,
fucked up and fucked over, but who's gonna trust us?
They labeled us criminals, convicts, offenders,
But you can't offend us–I'll never surrender.
Public defenders are public pretenders.
Now who in hell will defend us?

Gifts

Moises Colon

On my ride to jail
I thought I'll never see
                    the light of day again.
Sorrow and sadness, solitude and stress
                    but repress all that pain.
Today, I realize hope's not lost,
I've gained so much,
it all turned out to be a gift,
and now, I have much to give.

Trail

Andre Rivera

I am feeble and broken.
I groan because of the turmoil of my heart.
I am a mute who does not open his mouth,
like a deaf man who cannot hear,
a blind man who sees only the dark.

But since taking this class,
I've heard words kick-start
and fly like striped bass
–they come from my heart
–and this poem, My Ride to Jail,
is a whole new trail.

5. My First Night in Jail

I often wake up in the night, and I like to have something to think about.
–Marilyn Monroe

It is always consoling to think of suicide: in that way one gets through many a bad night.
–Friedrich Nietzsche

Come nightfall, the spirit of a defiant offender may still be strong. There's no denying, however, that the flesh has been delivered into a cage; it is literally impossible to escape that fateful fact. No wonder the confined night mind concocts dreams and dreads more vivid than the day itself. Questions confound the quest for sleep. Am I a name or a number? Is this a dead end–or am I on a journey? Who are these people? What is happening? What *will* happen? Am I in danger? Do I even dare to sleep? The hope is that sleep will soothe the raveled sleeve of care. Alas, however, come that first morning, even the day itself may seem like night, and every exertion the mere continuation of a hopeless dream. Does another life lie ahead? Or maybe merely slow death. For sure there will be time to ponder all such troubling questions.

The Scales of Justice

Joseph Birch

To win love and tip the scales
I blaze crazy-daring trails
but all this fails
and America's solution
                is to tuck me
                into jails.

Nightfall

Rudy Bisnauth

If I was a blind man, this I would know:
Nightfall, nightfall, just took its toll,
warmth is gone, wind's blowing cold,
birds stopped chirping, sounds down low.
If I was a blind man, this I would know:
Nightfall, nightfall, just took its toll.

The Beginning of Time

Neville Wells

So cold and uninviting.
Effectively naked.
My feelings drift,
shift harshly,
                crushed and marshy.
Need to heal.
Father Time offers a meal:
Tick Tock
                Tick Tock
                        Tick Tock.

Freeze

Rudy Bisnauth

Hands behind your back.

Step in, step out,
walk straight,
go left, go right.

Step in, step out,
look straight,
look left, look right.

Step in, step out.
Get undressed,
Get dressed.
Step in, –Yo!
When do I step out?

Morning delivers a hot summer day,
and me to metal bars and walls
where prisoners play.
Chatter through solid gates,
where imaginations tell tales.
Roaming visitors pass your grate.
Evil stares calculate your fate.
Toilet and sink, positioned, same place.
Iron bed, inches away.
Two phones, for, like,
a hundred motherfuckers.
I swear this is a land for suckers.

Predators and Prey

Sheldon Arnold

I remember like it happened yesterday. It was summer break and I was carefree. I'd worked all summer and I'd just gotten paid. I bought a new pair of sneakers and a new leather jacket. I was proud of myself. I couldn't wait to get back to school to show off this new stuff. On my way home a street gang approached me. They wanted my sneakers and jacket. I wasn't going to part too easily with what I'd earned. Words escalated into a fight. The gang leader drew a knife and stabbed me and I got rushed to the hospital. I realized then that evil exists and that the world was made up of predators and prey. To survive I needed to pick a side. I bought my first gun and made a promise to protect myself and my family from predators. But as time passed I realized I wasn't playing defense anymore. Now I was on offense. I'd become what I despised, a predator. I tried to tell myself that I was only robbing hustlers and drug dealers, but deep in my heart I knew I was wrong. Robbing eventually led to killing and the more I did of that, the easier it became. All too soon I wound up in Central Bookings.

Where the hell am I?
Why am I here?
What's that god-awful smell?
Doesn't anyone care?
Does anyone hear?
Is anyone here?
No! Just me in this box,
facing all these years.

Home Free

Andre Rivera

Home free—that's me!
It was a plan that could not fail.
But then sirens in the distance began to softly wail.
A trail of bread crumbs must have led them,
clues I'd left had spelled out mayhem.

I wept and choked on air so stale,
a criminal mind, how did I fail?
I woke up at midnight, sweaty and pale
within a dingy six-foot cell,
my high life had become my hell
and this was just first night in jail.

Plans for Me?

Ron Godbold

My first night in jail
I didn't sleep so well.
I couldn't understand
    why God took me
    from heaven to hell.
But sitting in that cell
who was I to tell?
It wasn't plain at all to see
the plans He surely had for me
    on my first night in jail.

Dales and Gales

Moises Colon

I was about to blaze a trail
when like a hammer smashing on a nail
or a body slamming on the third rail
I crashed to my first night in jail.

Everything in slow motion,
  moving like a snail.
Could not believe
  that I had failed.

Worst of all
I dreamed that night of Gale,
she of the sultry smile and tail,
and of how now
  she'd likely drop a veil
  for some local stud
  by the name of Dale.

Unafraid

Richard Moore

My first night in jail,
I was unafraid,
didn't give a damn.
The only thing I thought of
was to post bail.

I got into scraps,
kicked lots of ass,
–what's weird about that?
These were winning moves
back in my past.

But then I got convicted–"15 to 45," he called
I went straight to the big house
with the thickest concrete walls.
So, now I woke up and found myself in hell
And that's just the beginning
of my first night in jail.

Mail

William King

What, no bail?!
I'm a cowardly lion
with a tucked tail.
I'm scared like I seen a ghost,
skin white, almost pale.
Somewhere, somehow I have failed.
Can't sleep, cold and paranoid.
An orphaned kid who's lost his toys.
"Lights out," they cry, in a box jammed with men.
I wake in the night to pee in a cold, round tin.
At daybreak a uniform yells out, "Mail!"
And closes out my first night in jail.

6. Doing the Time

In jail a man has no personality. He is a minor disposal problem and a few entries on reports. Nobody cares who loves or hates him, what he looks like, what he did with his life. Nobody reacts to him unless he gives trouble. Nobody abuses him. All that is asked of him is that he go quietly to the right cell and remain quiet when he gets there. There is nothing to fight against, nothing to be mad at. A good jail is one of the quietest places in the world. Life in jail is in suspension.
–Raymond Chandler

To languish in a modern jail is to be supplied with three hots and a cot, have access to a library, work out in a gymnasium, receive and send mail, perhaps even to watch television. So where, really, is the punishment? So say the law-and-order crowd. The answer, of course, is that lengthy incarceration is a subtle and relentless form of early death. A short stint in jail can be a learning experience. Indeed, I often commend it to my friends. To serve serious time without the nourishment of hope and change, however, is only to be wished upon enemies. Isolation from loved ones then becomes akin to water torture. One may stoically deny the inner pain, but the remorseless dripping away of the days and nights atrophies both mind and heart. Most long servers are aware of the syndrome and make serious attempts to thwart it. "Do the time," they say, "don't let the time do you." But Father Time has never so far been arrested. Hence Dr. Seuss's question: "How did it get so late so soon? It's night before it's afternoon. December is here before it's June. My goodness how the time has flewn. How did it get so late so soon?" Happily, with the passage of time, brave long servers discover hidden treasures of the soul.

Freedom and Love

Josue "Big Bear" Pierre

I long to be free, come and go as I please.
To move about like a gentle breeze.
Oh, why did I scorn my liberties?

Will lockup in this steel bench press
remove the guilt within my chest?
My shame inflicts extreme duress,
is there a way to convalesce?
Am I crazy, a mental mess?
What if my crime I could repress?
Would that ever ease my stress?
Please, I pray you, grant me rest.

What my heart wants, I cannot touch.
Our bodies are separated by miles and luck.
I am concealed by a clouded wall of steel.
What if I chisel my way out?
Would I be too late?

You moved away.
I yearn for your touch.
Where is the love that covered me?
It was meant to live on
both far and near
but simply disappeared.
Shall I wait for it to re-appear?

You wanted to have my baby?
What happened to that?
Your love drives me crazy,
I want to blow away my brain.
To love them all is to love none at all.
That is why I truly love you with my all.

Without your love I am not much.
I'll haunt you from behind this wall.
Maybe I'm just a fool in love, my love.
But not to be fooled by love, my love,
is not to love at all.

I want to be free of you as you are free of me,
and yet to my dismay
your promises haunt my every day.
to love me till we're old and gray.
to love me to your dying day.

How come these memories refuse to stray
when so easily you turned and ran away?
Why do they wing above me like a bird of prey?
It's obvious you're the one who got away.

Why must I be tormented night and day?
It's obvious—right?—that I have things to say.
Why can't I live with shame and disarray?
Your love is greater than my shame, I say.

Why don't I just admit without delay
that I'm just a slave
who'll always love you,
even from the grave.

Hold That Thought

Joseph Birch

Hold that thought.
  Don't let it go away.
I went off without a plan,
  for years I had to stay.

Hold that thought.
  Don't let it go.
Time was flying,
  my thinking undying.
Hold that thought.
  Don't let it go.

Time moves fast.
For Why, for What,
  and to Where?
I have no idea.

Maybe Not

Moises Colon

I think, I think, I think. I think too much. I start all over. I redo it. I rebuild it. I rewrite it. I forget it. I do it halfway. I leave it alone. I come back to it.... I think, I think, and I think. I did it again.... That's my problem, over-thinking. That's my self defeating act. Or maybe not....

A Clean Plate

David Hutchings

Their census is senseless,
    we're trapped behind fences.
Barbed wire, hard wired, stuck in a mire
with black and brown faces.
It's basic, they're racist, so face it,
    we're back on that slave ship
    or working plantations
    with ten-year vacations.

There's just no escaping!
No peace and no justice,
the system is just us
shackled and trussed,
fucked up and fucked over
but who's gonna end this?
I'll never surrender.
I'll never surrender.
I'll never surrender.

Open the gate. I plan to escape.
A new date with fate and a clean slate.
A clean plate. Honeyed beans and a steak.
Maybe some brown rice.
Cold beverage with ice.
For now it's Jack Mack and Octo,
    whip it up in a hot pot.
Ninety degree heat's got me stuck
    in this steam box.
Only so much I can take.
I need to escape.
I need to escape.
Open the gate.

More to It

Rudy Bisnauth

There's more to it than cuffs and crackles.
More to it than pain and shackles.
More to it than days and nights.
More to it than oozing life.
More to it than parsing crime.
More to it than counting time.

I woke and saw that pain's a blessing.
Judgment Day is life's undressing.
Caress what is to be your rest;
love, in time, will be your test.

To me there is a whole lot more.
A door to open many tours.
More to it, I count my breath,
how many whispers might be left?

Insanity?

Josue "Big Bear" Pierre

If it is morally insane to kill or maim
to satisfy one's lusty desires,
which madman will avenge the slain
and purge the soul in devilish fires?

You've merely succeeded in causing distress.
Deliberate mindlessness makes no difference.
A man died in vain and you caused
another person
unimaginable pain.
Perhaps it brought you fame,
maybe even financial gain.
But in the end, all you've got
is a lifetime of disdain.
Someone cocks a head and asks,
How'll you drown that pain?
You wither in shame.

A Disc Jockey

William King

I was born with this gift,
    a good ear was all I had to give.
It began as a hobby then became a job,
    next thing you know I felt like a god.

I began to control people;
    I could make their heads nod,
    pull them into my orbit
    or free them to go.
    I could make them move fast
    or sometimes slo-mo.

Could make them smile, laugh, and shout,
    or leave them sad and down and out.
Could make them think positive or negative,
    but my goal was to share life
    and teach them to live.

09A5892

Josue "Big Bear" Pierre

Buried deep within this concrete skin
they say I am a savage and pin upon my thin
green suit the markings of the beast.
All I ever wanted was to eat, at least;
instead I have become the feast.
How will I be remembered?
Will I ever be, indeed? Emblazoned as I am
with the colors of the beast.

Blinded by layers of impenetrable grease
will this maddening darkness never cease?
Can I flee this numbing slumber
having worn this branding number?
Am I shadowed by my green fleece
having once resided in the belly of the beast?

I was a rebel without a cause,
but the time has come to pause,
perhaps to be my priest
and seek within the yeast
for the will to live and love
outside the innards of the beast.

And to a greater call,
I surely then will fall
loving those who have the least
inside these bowels of the beast.

7. Parole Hearings

There is nothing anyone can do anyway. The public has no power. The government knows I'm not a criminal. The parole board knows I'm not a criminal.
–Jack Kevorkian

The possibility of parole is intended to incentivize obedience among inmates, and thereby also quell the anxiety of the prison's most anxious occupant, the superintendent. The parole board typically comprises decent citizens with fine reputations. They are normally open to demonstrating compassion by releasing some deserving soul. Their underlying fear, of course, is that any mistake may come back to tarnish their own good names. My personal take is that while the odds of early release are inevitably low, lightning might just strike, and that at the very least a parole hearing is an opportunity to make a good impression, which may in turn, somehow, when least expected, lead to such a flash in the sky. Understandably, most who plead to the parole board for early release come with high hopes only to suffer rejection. Let that happen to you a couple of times and soon enough you'd find yourself sharing with the inmates the selfsame cynicism of the wit who noted that for bureaucrats procedure is everything and outcomes are nothing–and that if there is a way to delay an important decision, the good bureaucracy will find it.

Freedom Ride

Ron Godbold

Freedom! Freedom! The man he cried.
A tear-filled face showed the pain inside.
Oh how he wished he could see outside,
And know again that freedom ride.

Landslide

William King

I was young and high, give me a break,
it was terribly wrong, my fatal mistake.
A mishap opened the door to death,
a landslide of years left me struggling for breath,
and praying for mercy in the aftermath.
I learned a terrible lesson, as I trust you can see,
growing to manhood in this facility.
Scornful dismissal–a poison injection
entered my heart with parole rejection.

The Blender

Neville Wells

Truth was told. Nothing resolved.
Deaf ears, filled with fears.
Political agenda life up for tender.
Daughters tears, no time for sneers.
Put it in a blender, and mend her.

Who can talk to a deaf ear?
How can I come near
when you live in fear?
When you're ready to listen
my words will glisten
not end in the cistern.

How It All Went Down

David Hutchings

I'm a criminal, as all ya can see.
Car thief, drug dealer, stickup kid
 –that's all me.
Credit cards, mail fraud,
 even forgery.
Jaywalking and vandalism,
there was no crime
 too small for me.
I'm a criminal, as all ya can see.
I promise I won't do it again.
So you can safely set me free.
Hey, Yes! I've seen the light
 –so set me free.

You're not remorseful or even resourceful.
You're not even thoughtful.
Matter of fact you're awful;
 a criminal, convict, and offender
 who brags to us that he'll never surrender.
You're not sorry for what you got caught for.
Not even sorry for the thing you went to court for.
For a small price–your life–police, D.A.'s and judges,
 got bought for.
What the hell do you think we fought for?

The Past

Josue "Big Bear" Pierre

It is unfair, these days, to judge me
    by my long-lost ways.
That was then and this is now.
I was a crazy, immature child
until, within, here among men,
I found my own inner man
who compels me to be
        an even better man
and therefore no longer a vexation
        to my fellow man.
Better to be praised for righteous endeavor
        in the here and now,
than be judged for past misdeeds,
        and deemed unfit to reenter
        and take a bow.
So I inhabit the Inferno of Dante
with society's rejects and vigilantes.
How much better to dine on love
        with color-blind sinners
than to sour on rejection
        by soul-dead winners.

Perspectives

Richard Moore

I will never understand or accept
my parole rejection.
No one's cared for my growth
in this house of correction.
Sixteen years! Offenders and officers
attest to my changes,
yet here I sit to be judged
by three odd strangers.
Their minds on my crime,
they view me as danger,
a wild bird in a cage,
a dog in a manger.
They never can see inside of me
and so they never
set me free.

Clarity

Moises Colon

You do not know me.
You might as well leave right now.
You see on your sheets
merely a fraction of my past misdeeds.
They do not define me and neither can you.
You can neither judge me, dictate my destiny,
nor navigate my soul.
You may condemn, humiliate, persecute,
or even execute,
but nothing in your role is so noble
as you may imagine.
So, sure, reject me, then glance to floor.
I'll dismiss you from mind
as I head for the door.
I will move on, strong and proud,
and yet—*get this*—humble within;
untarnished by arrogance,
as you may doubtless avow.

The Reason for My Parole Rejection

Andre Rivera

I was about to be released and my reflection
on my waiting woman gave me an erection.

I had a speech written down to perfection
to mention my guilt was out of the question.

While patiently waiting to begin my session
I heard one of them whisper,
    "This asshole wasn't even a selection."

That barb felt like a truth injection
    so I told him to go fuck himself,
    and that was the reason
    for my parole rejection.

Myrmidon*

Joseph Birch

Upon following my brain,
I denied my conviction.
Focusing on the pain.
The parole board replied, Rejection.
That word struck like a myrmidon.
How can I save myself
            from another such setupon?

**Homer's* Iliad *records that Myrmidons were the fiercest warriors in all of Greece.*

Plans

David Hutchings

Stuck in this hellhole for another two years,
The parole board hit me, but really, who cares?

Man, I got plans, big plans.
These cats can't stop my shine.
It's just another setback
but they can't stop my grind.
Due to the nature of your crime.
What the fuck does that mean?
I already did my time!
It means they're pissed,
because I wouldn't drop a dime.

But if you choose, either way, you lose.
Go out like a bitch and be labeled a snitch.
No way, no sir—I cannot wear those shoes.

I walk upright, head high,
I'm a man, remember,
and I got plans—big plans.

You have your little scheme
but you can't end my dream,
you can't stop this thing.

This is just a minor setback.
It's a temporary delay,
you'll discover that, just wait,
I will see my day.
In the meantime I will pray.

Future Plans

Rudy Bisnauth

You turned me down?
I guess I don't understand
what you understand.
So I guess I gotta talk
to another man.

With a plan to make a new plan
I'll surely be dealt the right hand.

I'll make a new move to some new dudes,
who will choose for me a win this time
not a lose.

Okay then, because I lost,
I'll pursue the right moves,
and this time maybe you'll lose
–and then I'll be smiling again.

PART TWO

Surviving the Bullet & Breaking Free

The heart is the only
broken instrument that works.
–T. E. Kalem

Only by understanding a predicament can we see a way out of it. Right now, the dilemma is the yearning for freedom while incarcerated inside a concrete penitentiary. But forget about bars, walls, and wires. In fact, *all prisons are mental and emotional prisons.* They lock from the inside and we hold the key–so only we can let ourselves out. And we can do that. Yes, really. First, though, we need to understand the forces that pitched us into this wretched conundrum. With that in mind, let's consider the hidden meanings within a couple of great poems–*Snakebite* and *The Beautiful Lady Without Mercy.* Then let's move on to real-world poems about the snake that bites children, and the merciless lady who delivers men into hell.

8. Snakebite

Snakebite, a superb sonnet by contemporary poet Max Phillips, is our stepping-off point. It shows, better than any teacher ever could, that a deadly poison can enter the heart during childhood—thereby setting a course for tragedy. This big idea can set us on the path to liberation. Note the word *lash* in the opening line, A *lash of brightness catches you off guard in childhood.* Something bad happens to an innocent child and the world changes; *turmoil . . . plies her fangs of difference through your heart.* The child feels *different* in a bad way—weird and alienated. But here's the real problem: the kid doesn't quite realize what just happened! Doesn't know or dismisses it, says it was *nothing.* But, no, it was *something.* And it was something *bad.* And the last two lines come with the kicker: *You will not understand, but will endure, / snakebit, and never dreaming of a cure.* The child grows to adulthood. Then, mysteriously, or so it seems, life goes off the rails. Check out the poem below, then turn the page to see how the venom enters the heart and infects real lives.

A lash of brightness catches you off guard
in childhood. It completes you. You change size
in dreams of smelly water, catch your eyes
impersonating something bright and hard
as sun and moon wear hot grooves in the sky
and you lurch toward conclusion. Here your strange
illumined limbs betray you. You must change
unrestingly now. You, swollen and sly,
must welcome turmoil as a central friend
who plies her fangs of difference through your heart.
And now you're anyone's to take apart.
And now you're anyone's to find and mend.
You will not understand, but will endure,
snakebit, and never dreaming of a cure.

Venoms

Rudy Bisnauth

All snakes bite, but not all are poisonous.
Some strike to elude from fear, some only their prey,
some quiet, some loud, brave and without fear.
Damn this hurts–his fangs make me
his fond repast.
If I'd not stepped into his path, I'd not be here.
Such fear, roaming there in his grass, will I last?
My destination–oh what a task.
I'm lost emotionally but, I'm here.
I figure my destiny is rare,
mystical, yet typical, choices to make and take.
I try hard not to be physical.
Damn this hurts, maneuvering this deadly path,
slow never fast–my first and hopefully my last.

Scars

Sheldon Arnold

The system convicts,
freedom is stripped.
My inward eye
sees the sins I commit.
The burden is heavy,
I carry it with me,
these scars in my heart
from the snake that bit me.

Punctures

David Hutchings

I'm feeling light-headed,
nausea, hot flashes, chills rack my body.
I tremble and ache.
Whatever's wrong?
Why so weak do I feel?

I spy two puncture marks;
I've been bitten by the eel.

The poison runs within my blood,
anxiety, paranoia, heartbeat racing
to escape the coils of the beast.

But the venom courses through my veins
and now I'm in the tank
toppled by some Jezebel,
some lowdown, dirty skank.

Drugs

William King

I grew up round a family of thugs
who did whatever they needed to
    to get their drugs.
They sold drugs to get more drugs,
    sold their own clothes,
    video games and rings,
    even sold the baby's things.
The stole from their mom,
    even when she
    hid it in her tits.
Sisters and brothers too,
    anything, anyone
    to get their next hits.
I saw that crack's a powerful prey,
a creature I could never touch
    or sell to get my way.
I watched too many victims
    get bitten by this snake.
They tried to get the venom out
    but all too late.

Stakes

Neville Wells

Surgeon's scalpel, dissects a life.
Lonely child, open wound.
Locked forever in a deathly tomb.
He soothes his pain with alcohol.
Will he ever reclaim his soul?

Bars of illusion,
  the hardest to break.
Childhood confusion
  life at stake.

Oblivion

Moises Colon

I'm an adrenaline junkie.
I never chose it, it chose me.
I never knew it was an addiction
    until too late;
I never knew there was a snake
    until too late.
It slithered upward silent in attack.
How could I know that,
    until too late?
How could I know without knowing
    from the start?
I never knew the snake that bit me,
never saw fangs, never felt the venom
    enter my heart.

Tears

Andre Rivera

Why does the child weep in the middle of the night?
Is he hungry or soiled? Did he have a bad dream?
Does he cry for his mother to come to find out?
He grows to manhood and cries again.
Did he lose his job? Break with his lover?
Did a father, mother, sister, or brother pass away?
The tears turn to anger, the anger to rage.
Maybe he lost hope and faith–whatever
–he feels aflame, volatile;
did he drain a bottle of ether?

The rage subsides. Focused now, he sees more clearly.
He opens his mind and thinks.
No, it wasn't a premonition; it was a reality check.
He exited a drug-ridden mother's womb.
Fatherless, he survived a lack of schooling.
He gathered master's degrees in the ways of the streets.
He learned that vicious circles hate to stop spinning.
He vowed to his son that history would not repeat.
But now he's arrested and entombed,
and his son is strapped to the spinning wheel.
That's why the child weeps in the middle of the night.

Farewell

Joseph Birch

Dogs that bark never bite.
The snake that bit me was out of sight,
invisible by day, visible by night,
it moaned as it doused my inner light;
it lies there dead, now I see right.

Acorns

Kenneth Johnson

One from the flock,
a chip off the old block,
locked in a prison of DNA
beneath a poisonous overlay
that forms my thoughts, my feelings,
　　　　the things I say
creating a world of dismay, in disarray
that permeates every fiber of my being;
the blood in my veins that flows
from the top of my head
to the tip of my toes
letting me know
no matter where I hide
it will always show
until I find the courage to let go
of the bittersweet residue
that creates this lack of self-value
which all adds up to
　　　　I'm just like you, Dad.
Your arrant rejection and denied affection
Inflict my reflection with utter dejection.

You always broke your promises:
–when you were doing well
　　　　you stayed away from us;
–when you were doing bad, here you cometh
　　　　with your mental and physical abuse
saying things like, I'll never add up to nothin',
　　　　that I'm of no Goddammed use.

I don't know why Mama couldn't cut you loose.

All you ever did was lie.
It made you proud when Mama cried.
You had that lady petrified.
You'll never know how many times
I wished you'd died.

The only times we had good cheer
you played me like a puppeteer
and made me pull a joint, or down a beer.
Then, when I got high
and showed confusion and fear,
you laughed 'til tears flowed freely
from your eyes.

I'd have done anything to get your attention.
–You say you didn't realize?
–You say you're taken by surprise
to find me doing smoke
and dope and coke.
–You're not laughing.
–You don't get the joke?

You say *I* ran amok,
and when I remind you of those moments
you sneer that that's just my hard luck
and you tell me you don't give a fuck
and then you hold your pants
and you tell me what to suck.

Oh, no–you've nothing to explain,
so, why should you admit to shame
when you're the one who's not to blame?
Ever wonder why I hold you in disdain?

When you look at me
it's like you're staring in the mirror;
manifestation–things are so much clearer:

you hate yourself, and that's a clue
why you can't love me—because
I'm just like you, Dad.

Then came the day you gave me my first gun.
"Protection" for your only son, was what you said;
well, image fixed and damage done.
I started dissing everyone
I waved that gun and people
broke into a cockeyed run,
or froze and trembled
in their finest clothes.

And then, one day, to prove
I was a man, like you,
I shot—

Well, when those bullets spat
I fast became the coolest cat.
The police my jazz could never quell,
I led them on a hop through hell,
until the night they trapped me
in a dark motel,
trashed me with a fond farewell,
and tossed my bruised and broken body
to the steel hotel
where I awoke
to find myself
beside you
in the flanking cell.

So, Mama's words proved all too sad,
You're like your dad, was what she said.
Yeah, she foresaw the switcheroo,
and wept, predicting what she knew
—I'd surely end up
just like you, Dad.

9. The Merciless Lady

John Keats died at age 25, so never got to see his tale on the facing page, *La Belle Dame sans Merci—The Beautiful Lady Without Mercy*—claim top-ten ranking among the world's most popular poems. It tells of a traveler who meets a lost and sickly knight-at-arms on the side of a wintry hill. The sojourner asks, O *what can ail thee?* The knight wanly replies, *I met a Lady in the meads.... And sure in language strange she said "I love thee true."* In fact, her promise of true love was a lie. The strangeness of her love lay in her foreknowledge that his momentary bliss would be followed by his downfall. She seduces him and after making love he falls asleep and into a nightmare. In that last dream he ever dreams, the *starved lips* of her *death-pale* former lovers offer a *horrid warning—La Belle Dame sans Merci hath thee in thrall.* He wakes to find himself abandoned, adrift and dying on the side of the road. Perhaps the poem is popular because it is a universal parable. Perhaps we can each fall prey to such an enthralling and addictive so-called lady. If so, then a crucial step to survival is to identify and name the pitiless figure whose charms and wiles can lead to unhappy dreams within prison walls, where no birds sing. A bevy of such ladies appear on the pages that follow.

La Belle Dame sans Merci

The Beautiful Lady Without Mercy

—John Keats

O what can ail thee, Knight at arms,
Alone and palely loitering?
The sedge has withered from the Lake
And no birds sing! . . .
"I met a Lady in the Meads,
Full beautiful, a faery's child,
Her hair was long, her foot was light
And her eyes were wild.
She found me roots of relish sweet,
And honey wild, and manna dew,
And sure in language strange she said,
'I love thee true.'
She took me to her elfin grot
And there she wept and sighed full sore,
And there I shut her wild wild eyes
With kisses four.
And there she lullèd me asleep,
And there I dreamed, Ah woe betide!
The latest dream I ever dreamt
On the cold hill's side.
I saw pale Kings, and Princes too,
Pale warriors, death-pale were they all;
They cried, 'La Belle Dame sans Merci
Hath thee in thrall.'
I saw their starved lips in the gloam
With horrid warning gaped wide,
And I awoke, and found me here,
On the cold hill's side.
And this is why I sojourn here,
Alone and palely loitering;
Though the sedge is withered from the Lake
And no birds sing."

Have Another

David Hutchings

Have another, she said. Well I just might! Coors Lite and Red Stripe. Saint Ides and Pauly Girl. Budweiser, Schlitz, and San Miguel. Ballantine Ale and Pink Champale. Colt 45 and Miller High Life. Red Bull, Pabst Blue Ribbon. Malt Liquor and Heineken, Foster's, Amstel, and Corona. On every block and every corner. Crazy Horse and Midnight Dragon, 211's and King Cobra. Never seen a day sober; drank myself into a coma. Crack the bottle, catch the aroma, see it rise and sweetly foam up. Pour out a lil' for the homies that ain't here–this ain't beer. This here is my elixir–some evil concoction I just mixed up. St. Ides and Guinness Stout–we call that eight ball. Man, I'm so smashed, I can feel my face fall. Some call me an alky, others call me a lush, but I don't give a fuck–just pour me another cup; I'll get more twisted than yesterday, with just a little luck. Got dead drunk and blacked out, no Ifs and no Buts, woke up, remembered nothing, puke my guts, face down in the toilet bowl, man this really sucks. I beg the Lord for mercy; Never again, I cry, then swear amends. Later that night I'm back on the corner with my happy-hour friend.

Encounters

Andre Jones

When I was sixteen I was introduced to a beautiful lady by family and friends. She was well acquainted with everyone I loved and trusted, so it was easy for me to embrace her. The more intimate we became, the more I knew she wasn't no good for me. As they say, if you love something too much it could be no good for you. But I loved her to the point that whenever she was around I would act out, disrespecting my family and friends, harassing and fighting people–and breaking the law, often, just to always have her around. I cannot lie though: she always made me feel good when we was together, so I thought. But when she wasn't around and I came back to reality, I was able to see the effect of her being around me. One day I sat down and told her we couldn't be intimate no more. I gave her two reasons for splitting: one, I'm a father now and my daughter's gonna need my attention more than anything; and, two, every time I'm around you everything in my life goes wrong. She understood, or so I thought. We went our own ways for a while. But when an obstacle got in my way I would go for a walk to clear my head, and there she would be, waiting with soothing words, and wanting to befriend me. Some nights I would take another path to stay out of her way. One night a friend of mine called my home and invited me to dinner at his house. As I entered his door, there she was sitting at the table, beautiful as ever. Over dinner our eyes locked and we began to talk. Then she kissed me and I kissed her back. We got passionate, ignored everyone else, and became intimate that night. Then a fight broke out with my friend and I got involved. When I woke up next morning, I was lying in a jail cell trying to remember what happened the night before.

"What am I doing here?" I asked the officer outside my door.

"You murdered someone last night," he said, deadpan.

"What happened to the lady that was with me?"

"She left with a couple of other guys when she knew you was going to jail for the rest of your life."

"She just left me here?"

"We asked her if she was your wife or girlfriend, but she just laughed in our faces. 'No, I don't even remember his name,' she said, 'I just met him tonight.'"

Miss Vanity Glamour

Neville Wells

When I was young and debonair,
I courted her, she seemed so fair;
beguiling eyes and golden hair,
and teasing lips–and do I dare?
Alas, I tossed aside all care
and sought to tame this flying mare;
imbibing every potion fair
we trysted in her lover's lair
–until without a backward glance or care
she vanished–and to my despair
I woke to suck on prison air
within a cell without a prayer.

Cool Cat

Joseph Birch

I thought I had it down pat
when I set out win that dame
by being a Cool Cat.
But it didn't swing like that
and I've no one to blame;
I'm a tomcat who lost his hat.
That mirror mate sealed my fate.
Twelve to life–nothing's cool about that.

Life Awaiting Death

Richard Moore

We're born into this beautiful lady called life.
Then we find out about death,
where we're all headed.
As children don't understand,
so we begin to think about it, maybe once,
and then for some of us
maybe twice.

The Poisoned Well

Andre Rivera

The beautiful lady without mercy
aroused the blood in my good friend Percy.

No, no, I said, something's off—I wasn't joking.
You're jealous, he said, so stop cock blocking.
I laughed and left it like that.

I got a night call and opened my eyes a crack.
It was Percy's number! Was the sex out of whack?
I grabbed the phone. He screamed in pain,
My nuts ache like they've been hit with a bat.
I laughed and asked him where he was at.

I got there and he scratched
like a dog with fleas.
Whatever's wrong?
It burns when I pees.
Tell me you used a condom, Percy.
His wide eyes said,
No—I gotta disease.

Percy, Percy, Percy, Percy!
That's what you get
for being so thirsty
and dipping yourself inside the well
of the beautiful lady without mercy.

SAW

William King

What I'm about to say to your open jaw
might cut your life in half like never before.
This is why I call it SAW.
We all have a weakness, and sex was my flaw.
I forgot about work and stopped going to school.
I wasn't thinking but I thought I was cool.

Okay, okay, I thought sex was my all,
But I still needed to find a way to blend in,
so I took a hard look at alcohol.

Wow! Now I was fearless and happily numb
till I started to shrink, from forgetting to eat,
so I found a way back: they call it weed.
Now my boring life was brain-dead fun
so I never knew I'd become so dumb.

Blind to the world, I crashed to the floor;
blind to the world and my every need;
blind to the world, this was all I SAW:
S for sex, A for alcohol, W for weed.

PMS

Joseph Birch

Beauty was her disguise.
Lack of mercy was my surprise.
She seduced and betrayed me
right in front of my eyes.
The Beautiful Lady with PMS.
Pain, Misery, and Suffering.
One hell of a prize.

Streetwise

David Hutchings

For me, the cold, heartless, unforgiving Beautiful Lady was New York–and the streets that berobed her. As a boy they were always calling me, and soon enough they hooked me. Such beautiful sounds: sirens, gunshots, people yelling and cussing, fighting and arguing, bottles being broken. Such sounds doubtless deter some denizens. "Man you hear all those gunshots and carrying on I ain't going out there." Not me, to whom it was all a sweet serenade, the loveliest lullaby ever sung. I became a slave to its rhythm. I was drawn to the flashing lights like a gull to an eel, especially on hot summer nights, when game is afoot. Daytime's different: the streets are crowded with everyone rushing back and forth to work or shopping. But the sun goes down and the lights come up. Now you see the action. Now you see the hustlers, the pushers, the pimps, the junkies, the hoes, the addicts, the con men. They were all superheroes to me. Their lifestyle had me mesmerized. As a teen, on hot summer nights, I cruised the streets with my friends until the wee hours. Then came the day my mother locked me out. You never come home and you love the streets, she said, so now they're yours. But this was great! Now I could party forever. It was cool with me. But then the seasons shifted. Suddenly everybody's going to school, shopping, getting all freshed up. And I'm still wearing the same clothes I wore all summer. It's hard to keep up at school when you're homeless. Homework is hard when you got no home. How do you show up at school when last night you slept on a roof, or in someone's car? Who do I turn to for help? I turn to the streets. The streets showed me how to survive. They taught me how to deal drugs. And to lie and to steal and to rob. They drugged me and put me on the road to prison. When I woke up the streets had disappeared. Now there were only walls. Fuck the streets. You can have that bitch to yourself. I just want to go home.

Jezebel

Herburtho Benjamin

In the wake of dreaming from what it seemed,
Jezebel came on to thee timely. In the midst of ease,
swaying her fanny, as hot as a heat wave, luring me
to succumb to her feet, for her ever growing needs,
relentless in her approach to devour the strongest,
the means for her to live the longest.

Fake Friends

Sheldon Arnold

Hanging out with fake friends,
hoping the means justify the ends.
By any means necessary
                to keep up with new trends.

Never went to go to bed at night;
instead would party, rob, and fight.
This was it—*Man I'm living the life!*

Turned out I only thought I was living
and now I'm pissed off in this prison.
But I see the need for my acts so shady;
impressing fake friends—merciless ladies.

Could You Be Love

Josue "Big Bear" Pierre

In Central Park on a spring afternoon a 5'5" brown-eyed, thick in the thighs, lovely sister smiled. Hi, cutie, she said. I blushed and closed my eyes and turned her image in my mind. I thought, so this is it, love at first sight. But when I looked up, she'd disappeared. I nearly stumbled over an elderly couple, describing her to them. They said they'd seen her around the corner, and if hurried I'd catch her. But be careful, the old man said, she has an evil twin sister. I raced to the corner. She was nowhere in sight. I asked a middle-aged couple if they had seen her. They said she was sitting by the pond a little way on. Once you catch her don't let her go. Sure thing, I said, and hurried off to find my one true love. As the sun was setting I happened upon a young teenage couple and described her to them. Yeah sure we know her, she's our home girl, but you better hurry because she's about to leave the park. But cut through the lane called Lovers Stroll and you'll run right into her before she leaves. I turned and ran through that winding upward path, and there she was just up ahead. I called to her but she didn't hear. A stranger caught her attention for me. I confessed I'd been chasing her most of the day, that she truly was love at first sight for me. She shot that same smile. That's my sister, she said. We look the same, but we're as opposite as night and day. Her name is Love and she's not for you. But I'm Lust, and I'm here right now, will I do?

10. Visiting Day

I never saw a man who looked
with such a wistful eye
upon that little tent of blue
we prisoners call the sky,
and at every careless cloud that passed
in happy freedom by.
—Oscar Wilde

In prison it becomes as clear as the white clouds that trail so wistfully above the yard, that a visit from a loved one is the surest sign that someone cares, that one's feelings of loss, longing, and love are shared. A tragedy of New York prison life is the distance the loved one typically has to travel to share that affection. Then comes the embarrassment of entry. Like a haughty *maitre d'* in a snooty restaurant, sniffy front desk officials sometimes equate visitors with criminals. Some of those imagined interlopers may well be ex-offenders, but what the hell? Courtesy freely given is a precious gift, especially to these ever-troubled souls prepared to remove their shoes and belts, and empty their pockets before stepping through the X-ray machine. Finally, the first leg of the journey is done, and the inmate comes into view. What a moment of truth that is. The prison jumpsuit tells a story, as may shackles, too. How lucky are they who can embrace and touch, listen and whisper. No matter what an eavesdropper may hear, the underlying pain of those who meet within prison walls is always evident.

Reflections

Sheldon Arnold

Hours of joy, end in depression.
When we get up and head off in different directions.
My mother, my father, my wife and kids
without my protection are gone in an instant;
they disappear, time is distance, missing years.
Searching for my soul, I look in the mirror.
It's deadly clear that no one's there,
just the ghost of the boy I was.
But maybe I'm stressing, not getting the lesson.
Yeah, right. And so now
I'm lost in contrition.
Oh, how I miss them.

Reunion

Neville Wells

Butterflies float, a belly of jelly.
Prison halls, dark and smelly.
Worse than you see on the telly.
Open door, bright light, chest tight.
Daddy! Daddy! yells little tyke.
She floats like a kite, her arms bite,
she holds on tight.
Still some fight, enough to last
another night.

Embraces

Josue "Big Bear" Pierre

Even after all these years
visiting day, I must say,
can leave me in tears.

To see loved ones I first strip naked
and consent to be degraded.

Needless to say
to embrace the faces
who journey the day
to this cold chalet
come in answer
to what I pray.

Being with those I love is joy
but too soon time flies,
then comes goodbye.

Moments

David Hutchings

On this day, I look my best;
    fresh dressed, nicely pressed,
    hair sharp, beard tight.
    A dab of cologne? No contest.

A C.O. slips me my guest room pass.
I'm out the door, gone–loved ones await.
Hugs and kisses, *I miss you so much.*
Hands soft to the touch caress my face,
and my mind drifts to another place.

Look how much the kids have grown.
Boyyee, you been working out?
                Your muscles showing!
                Maybe a little.
Nephew's on my lap,
                I tickle,
                he wiggles,
                we all giggle.

Sis's eyes swell with tears,
I wish you were at home, she says.
In that second,
                I truly felt alone.

Evasions

William King

The morning rises, my mouth's cotton dry.
As they call my name others look, as if it's fame.
I wait in a room of anxious men,
for a jumper-suit that fits,
Velcro-lined within.
A buzzer brays as a door opens slowly.
Here comes my family, I'm no longer lonely.
Two hours fly. They stand, all homely
then as expected comes the query,
How long must you now stay, oh dear one?
I contemplate a soft evasion
but then in truth I say,
God willing, I'll be here no longer
than next visiting day.

Great Discussions

Richard Moore

Today was a great day.
I saw my family.

We shared some things,
ideas and opinions,
deeds and smiles;
we needed that,
after all this while.

Some moments passed with little to say,
mostly though, great discussions,
word by word, and one by one,
came from nowhere into play,
and we enjoyed a really great day.

Fatherhood

Moises Colon

I cannot remember how long
                I longed for this day,
but I do remember the rate of my heart
and the thousand thoughts and all the things
                that I would say.
When I saw the vibrant youth-filled face,
the one I've yearned to embrace
                ever since my fall from grace.
I was the happiest dad in the human race
                on this, my first visiting day.

First Impressions

Andre Rivera

The C.O. calls with rousing news,
A female's here to visit you.

In less than half an hour
I soap and shower
and brush my teeth removing any taste
she might find stale or sour.
I slip into my clean green outfit,
so I can look exquisite,
then splash a dash of Muslim oil
but not so much as to cause
my manly scent to spoil.

I wait at the gate, then comes my officer escort.
I ask if he knows of any handy candy
that might by me be bought.

She's at the table, a sweet white stork,
but worried, like I have scared her;
as she looks away I curse the day
and the jerk who fucked up the paperwork
–I am the wrong Rivera.

Okay

Joseph Birch

Visiting day was my wish;
I didn't need to pray.
I merely wished to see if things
might just play out my way.

She hoped she could stay.
I didn't need to pray.
When she softly stepped away
I got to feeling
that things would be okay.

Voices

Rudy Bisnauth

Anticipating your wait,
all these hours,
finally feels great.
Here and now,
hugging, caring,
eyes all brimming,
lovers staring.
You must know I miss you?
I figure that's why you're here.
How long did it take?
–scratch that–
I really don't care.
I'm just happy you made it,
overjoyed that you're here.
Just know I'll always love you
–and for you will always be here.

11. Black and White

Jesus was a poor black man who lived in a country and a culture controlled by rich white people!
—The Reverend Jeremiah Wright

This is Obama's pastor, folks! He chose this hatemonger as a spiritual leader.
—Rush Limbaugh

The profound mistake of Reverend Wright's sermons is that he spoke as if this country is still irrevocably bound to a tragic past. But what we know—what we have seen—is that America can change.
—Barack Obama

Since it is not founded on reason, prejudice does not respond to logic. What can turn racists into humanists, however, is a stint in prison. Here, where all men are intent upon survival, all races are equal. Disrespect can be downright dangerous. But only an idiot truly wants to fight, so civility and courtesy are qualities to be developed in oneself and prized in others. Yes, American prisons do indeed seem vastly overpopulated by deeply suntanned denizens. To be lily-white is not to be the norm. But look a little closer and you'll discover that just about every member of this rainbow coalition hails from the ranks of the socially and economically deprived. The moral—that it is not color but socioeconomic status that creates miscreants—is inevitably lost on white racists. But console yourself by glancing to the current Supremes—the justices, not the singers. They too showcase the blight of racism, black and white, reverse and straight. No, if you'd really like to experience the world of the truly enlightened, win yourself a spell in prison.

Chess Game

Rudy Bisnauth

Black or white, wrong or right?
Don't let the topic fool you,
'cos that's what it's meant to do.
It's like a game of chess, my friend,
 a passion to pursue,
 all based upon the way you move
 and what you choose to do.
Black or white, wrong or right,
let's all see how you move.

The Inner Chart

David Hutchings

Black and white makes gray,
some may say thoughts decay, go astray,
 seek to find a better day.
Some thoughts are trapped, some are free;
 but are they really? Do I need to pay a fee?

Can I speak my mind and not pay a price?
Can I truly say what I feel is right?
Can I talk of the fence between black and white?
But is there really a difference?
 Is one right and one wrong?
 Is one weak and one strong?
I shut my eyes tight, we all seem the same
 on the brain's inner chart.
Ah, but yes—what might set us apart,
 I now sense in your heart.

A Question

Joseph Birch

Sometimes things are tight.
Black and white
    one wrong look–a fight.
Black and white!
    Am I wrong? Are you right?
Who can tell from black and white?

Shades of Gray

Andre Rivera

Racism in the ghetto
    was just another day.
When it came to black and white
    there were no shades of gray.
I wised up to that jungle
    and tried to get away.
Hey, not so fast, the devil said,
    and I was shred and lay
    bleeding in a gutter
    with a bullet in my tray.
First I saw black
    then I saw white
    but never shades of gray.

Rainbows

Moises Colon

I am black, I am white, I am brown,
and to that rainbow I never frown.

I welcome every color in me,
all that I am,
and all that God
has made me to be.

The conquistador, the soul, and the heart,
I embrace every aspect and live every part.

Yes that's me–all entwined,
I can never see black or white
for I am color-blind
when my eyes prevail
–and color-blind
whenever I fail.

Bad Advice

Sheldon Arnold

As clear as day, they say, and as black as night
that the world is filled with black and white.
But they fail to see the facts of life
when all they see is black and white.
Just like dogs, they're imprecise
when all they see is black and white.
We all may fall to bad advice,
regardless of whether
we're black or white.

Brothers

Richard Moore

Black and white! They try to tell me
that we're different
and that one is better than the other.
But my brain's become deaf to "they"
'cos we're all brothers
with a different mother.

Progress

William King

Back then black and white
was the only thing in sight.
Right or wrong it was a fight.
Abraham that changed a law,
that freed the slaves but led to war.
Malcolm shattered the glass of race.
Then Martin followed with words and grace.
When all's said and done in the dark of night,
we go hand in hand when we turn on the light.
When the smoke cleared and the sky became bright,
we united and elected a president black
who is also white.

Wages

Neville Wells

It is neither here nor there,
life just is not fair.
Do or dare, we can end in the lair.
Be a bear and refuse to care.
You're from the loin, learn to join;
become a pair and earn the coin.

Black in the Hood

Josue "Big Bear" Pierre

What's up my Nigga? *A Yo! Watch yo mouth! Who you calling a "Nigga"?*

Nah, I'm not talking about the Down-South country cotton-picking Nigger.

I'm talking about the Up-North, New York City, Diddy popping, swag out Nigga!

Oh so there's a difference? Yeah, not that "mines and yours great-great-grandma, Yessir Master Nigger."

No, I'm talking about that "NWA—Nigga-With-an-Attitude, that Tupac I'd rather be an N, I, G, G, A so I could get-drunk-and-smoke-weed-all-day Nigga."

And in that case I'm that "N, I, G, G, E, R Nigger that's hated without cause, simply because of the Color-of-His-Skin Nigger. That Nat Turner, Frederick Douglass, MLK, Malcolm X Nigger."

That was then this is now. That hat-low, pants-sagging, tatted-up, hip-hop generation, White Boy calling himself "Nigga."

Well I'm an "Each-One Teach-One, am I my brother's keeper?, common, Talib Kweli, self-conscious type of Nigger."

Well I'm a "From the Hood Nigga. Never had a positive role model, gang banging, drug dealing, slingin' hard dick and bubble gum to these Nappy Head Hoes Nigga. Everything is owed to me. This is for 400 years of slavery."

Ain't no "Fortune 500 clean-cut, suit-and-tie Wanna be Somebody, doctor or lawyer lame-ass square-ass nigger in my family."

Oh, okay you one of those "Native Son, type of Nigga." Quick to rob, steal, and kill from your own, get angry blame Whitey, riot and burn your own neighborhood but don't really want no problems with the Man, will just call it "White Man justice. Black Man grief quick-to-fit-every-stereotype of Nigga."

Yeah that's right. And I know your kind too: "Proud to be Black, Free Your Mind, and the Rest will Follow. Return to the Motherland, black fist in the air, Black Panther where-are-they-now type of Nigger."

Well it's better than being one of those "hate my gums Because it's Black, Willie Lynch syndrome, never had to run from the Ku Klux Klan, but got to run from my own kind, type of Nigga."

I hate ya Niggas. Well we hate you too. "Uncle Tom Ass, Sambo, Yessir Master I'll be a Good House Nigger–fuck the Field Nigga." *Highly educated type of Nigger, that's what you are.*

Nope, but I'll tell you what we both are: a seventeen-year-old, unarmed young black man, and seen thru the eyes of like-minded George Zimmerman we're still just another "Nigger/Nigga."

Suntans

Josue "Big Bear" Pierre

If I were to step outside of my shoes,
and walk a mile with you,
would I know what it's like to be you?

It's true we have our differences
but I am actually a lot like you.

Would it be wise for us to set aside
whatever prejudice I seem to have about you?
Perhaps we may even learn a thing or two
being mere humans, you like me, and me like you.

Might it be, since I was born another shade than you
  that we cannot conceptualize
that beyond our suntans we share
  the selfsame inner hue?

So let's get civilized and come to realize
  that I'm actually just like you.

The Two of Us

Josue "Big Bear" Pierre

It's a self-defeating act when black kill black. All for the love of dealing crack. Some think it's fun to see a black man run from the barrel of his gun. But you've been misled by the lies that historians said, "You're cursed because your skin's been kissed by the sun."

Both you and me are the native sons of the original man. Brought to this foreign land where Indians used to run, united as slaves. But free we've become divided. How did this hypocrisy ever come to be, such a mockery? Whatever happened to our black pride?

Generation X, that's you and me, are lost to this cause. That pioneers died to set us free so that we may live in peace and harmony. I pray that generation next, continues to fight for this righteous cause.

For ignorance is never bliss, and hindsight is not always perfect. Why not strive for that almighty godly wisdom? I sit in awe, and reflect on Black and Latino faces, once considered minority, but now the majority.

Can't help but to think this is the action of a racist society, and not merely prison politics. But this is all part of their tricks. So that both you and I become another statistic. No longer my brother's keeper. Instead we kill over red and blue. Colors that represent neither me or you. Some say it's genocide when blacks ride to kill blacks, and scream out, "I'll murder you."

I pray that my warm heart never turns cold. Where I would be so bold. I kill my fellow man. From the land of my mother, all for the love of someone else's gold. For my soul is worth much more than diamonds and gold.

I pray to the sky up above to set my people free, from their mental slavery. But there must be some accountability from both you and me to stop this apocalyptic prophecy. I'd like to see all mankind live in peace and harmony. But some say that will never be.

Welcome to the Planet Earth.
Black and White,
North and South.
East and West.
Night and Day.
They all add up to Power of One
–You and I!
–The human race.
–Wake up people!

12. Phoenix Moments

"Swipe again!" The subway turnstile couldn't read my "smart" card and sourly urged me to Swipe Again—and Again, and Again. The crowd was pressing. My wife, her own card in hand, peered over my shoulder. The turnstile bar abruptly swung, hurtling us into the underground. Margaret, not grasping what happened, was drawn onto the escalator and vanished. "That woman with you didn't pay!" shouts a plainclothes officer. "You're under arrest! Where's your ID?" Alas, I had only a Metrocard, a theater program and a five-dollar note. I was cuffed, traipsed into the Broadway lights, and frisked. I attracted odd looks from subway hordes unused to seeing a silver-haired male restrained within a phalange of gun-toting cops. But not to worry. I was into my third year of running a half-day-a-week program for Rikers Island inmates. I figured I'd not meet anyone more sinister in a downtown cell. If you'd like the rest of that story you might enjoy my book, *How to Break Out of Prison*. Anyway, I shared that night with eighteen strangers in a tiny cell in the infamous Manhattan Tombs. Next morning, Margaret and I strolled out into a sunny, late-spring afternoon. The trees were green and birds were singing. I was relieved, exultant even. Freedom—never take it for granted. I stopped stock-still. "We're walking atop the Tombs," I said. Indeed, at that very moment, the wretched refuse of our gleaming shores, our truly needy, our tired and poor, neatly packed together within sturdy iron bars set into shimmering, freshly disinfected concrete floors, were huddled, hurting, and yearning to breathe free. Why am I telling you all this? Because whenever I depart a prison class, I feel that same mix of exhilaration and sadness. Exhilaration because every week I meet the nicest people and see what we all see: incredible renewal, inner growth that you can hear, and outer dignity that you can embrace. So every week I'm both exulted and sad to leave all that behind.

The Phoenix

Josue "Big Bear" Pierre

Past is past
but in memory
moments last.

If ignorance is bliss
hindsight's a gift
and guilt a graveyard shift
so retrospect shall be my shrift.

Moments pass too quick
but I've learned a simple trick:
Just as infants learned to crawl,
my kismet was to hit a wall,
but the rise is greater than the fall,
and soon enough I will stand tall.

From the sins that it despises
A Phoenix gently rises.

And this I heard the Phoenix say,
Fly on now, without delay.
Don't fear or fret, I heard it say,
the promised land's in your purvey,
obstacles just pave the way.
Continue on, I heard it say.

This bitter test is protein for your quest.
Yes, there are valleys to summon tears;
but there'll come peaks, these passing years.
Say thanks for everything you face,
your Higher Power fills the space
and sheds a universal grace
that you can tap to win the race.

I float above you riding high
in every sun and every moon
and every cloud that passes by.
So in cold nights or sunny days
I swear I hear the Phoenix say, *c'est la vie.*
A child asks why I sleep with hunger
and his mother may say, *c'est la vie.*
A wife contemplates suicide,
and she may say, *c'est la vie.*
An old man, ill, will pass away
and his son may say, *c'est la vie.*
An addict dying day by day,
may hear his dad say, *c'est la vie.*
A gangster bleeding in a quay
invites the blessing, *c'est la vie.*
In a life of care and disarray
I rise and with the Phoenix, say, *c'est la vie.*

My First Teacher

Joseph Birch

I learned life's lessons.
I learned I'm a blessing.
My first teach, she's my mother,
  a great preacher.

Big Brass

Richard Moore

I've noticed the government trying to repeal
what Mr. Edward Snowden was able to reveal.
But Big Brass credibility now merely squeaks
on account of all the law-breaking leaks
they're trying to conceal.

The Price of Gold

Sheldon Arnold

I sped through life not heeding
my preacher or even hearing
my mother's pleadings
until I blindly slipped and fell
and woke within this dark hotel.
For the price of gold, I lost my soul,
but within these walls I found myself
and then I saw that life itself
is cruise control and a manly role.
I've seen the light and I'll do what's right
now that love and not gold
is my true north,
my ever true magnetic pole.

The Wrong Ball

Rudy Bisnauth

Right or wrong my actions carry me on. The elevation, dedication, preservation, contemplation–I never did have any patience. Here are my structural defects in a modern pretext:

Lied to and trusting the wrong cause, I put two and two together, faced with many flaws; greed, lust, envy, all the wrong mixtures befriended me; hosted to the wrong ball, I knew this, but still craved the same call; not listening to peers, aggravated this fall.

Living with fears, holding back tears, yet still understanding my cares. Mixed emotions, placed me right out in the open. Chosen, to be picked, placed on front line. Wrong or right, I was always taught to fight. Lost in a war, but yet no battle scars.

But now I have new weapons–paper and pen;
with these I'll win–trust me, you'll see me again.

Standing for Nothing

Herburtho Benjamin

You stand for nothing.
The bottom is overcrowded.
The wealthiest city of unfulfilled dreams.

Moving up is the direction.
It's essential to transcend.
Seeing though darkness with a clear vision.

Doing for others as you'd like them to do for you.
Doing that for yourself, too.
Laying a trail like the martyrs before us.

My Self-Defeating Act

William King

My self-defeating act—it took me ten years
to figure out that.
I didn't take life seriously, everything for fun,
and that's a fact.
A physical feel-good, a mental high,
I thought this was good enough
to get by—or to fly.
Leaning on others,
never standing like a man.
I saw myself as "all that"
and became my number-one fan.

The judge gave me a football number
for an accidental kill
But when all was said and done,
I chose this time to make life real.
So I wake up every morning
with this guilt upon my back
and swear I'll never let it come again
—my self-defeating act.

Love and Lust

Josue "Big Bear" Pierre

They seem the same but are as opposite
as night and day.
Love is pure and warm and gentle and kind
and comforting on the coldest day.
Some thought they killed in their quest for love
but were merely blinded by lustful daze.

They mirror one another but are not the same.
Love's faithful and true and remains with you,
especially when you're sad and blue.
Lust rushes in but soon fades away.

Some spend a lifetime seeking love
but lust trips them along the way.
At the crossroad where desire meets lust
choose love's highway you surely must.

Manhood

Richard Moore

Friends told me that true strength
is the special gift of the physically strong.
But now I've come to realize,
that philosophy is totally wrong.

In the past I had the inkling
that providing for my family
by any means you can
makes a man.
But years in this weird land
showed another way of thinking
and now the definition of a man,
I truly understand.

True Story

Josue "Big Bear" Pierre

Once upon a time I lived a life of crime.
Always eager to turn a quick dime.
Why slave a whole week just to get mine?

Dealing drugs! Every Black Man's claim to fame
–would I not want the same?
A rush of quick money makes life worthwhile
and with addicts lining up by the mile
that moolah flowed like the River Nile.

Okay, I knew the other side of this.
Didn't take long. Somebody snitched.

But ask me now, and this I'll say:
you'll never find me dealing hay
not 'cos it doesn't pay,
not 'cos I'd wind up in a ditch.
No, because, truth to tell
it's a bitch of a life
and a sure road to hell.

To Be Continued

Andre Rivera

My self-defeating act began when I thought
school was whack,
You can be anything you want to be, whoever said that
should've been slapped.

Just like in *The Matrix* our minds are being hacked
to have me think my only option was to sell crack.

I paid bills and fed the family off that first stack,
my mind was made up, ain't no looking back.
To be continued was my self-defeating act.

But don't hold me to the sequel,
I'd rather leave this poem just like that.

Differences

Andre Rivera

While incarcerated I've learned to be passive and humble because of the segregation and racism that exists to this day, whether it's the officers, civilians, or even my own peers. I also learned to fall back and be observant because of the two sayings I go by. Keep your head above water so you can watch the sharks around you. And cut the grass short to your lawn to expose the snakes (which I think is kind of ironic because I live in the projects and we don't have a lawn—the whole sidewalk is concrete). My mother always told me, you know who your family and friends are when you're locked up. Which turns out to be true in many ways because a stranger you meet in here can wind up being your best friend for life. And the best friend you grew up with out there and have known for most of your life is really the stranger. To be honest I've learned we are no different from each other. Except the only thing that separates us is each other. We have a lot in common, just look at our backgrounds. Minorities in poverty in a so-called urban community—the ghetto. Raised by a single parent. Grew up around drugs, prostitutes, guns, and violence. Oh yes, some in the government know how to divide and conquer. But if we educate each other and stop the segregation and racism within, then we can overcome the oppressors who set up the crazy laws and sentencing guidelines that got most of us here in the first place—and are holding too many of us here right now. That's what I've learned.

13. Last Words

People will say, "there's heaven and hell," and they take it so serious that they look so sorrowful with penitence. I would rather ask them to show me the route that leads to heaven or hell.
–Michael Bassey Johnson

According to our Puritan forebears, the purpose of a penitentiary was to provoke *penitence*. This would be achieved by stripping the denizens of material possessions, confining them in solitary cells, and hooding their heads, thereby forcing them to journey inwards, contemplate their sins, and repent. But what is a journey without a friend to share it? We came into this class as strangers but soon became comrades. Poetry put hearts and souls on display. Secret lives were bared. Uncensored confessions were heard. Did penitence follow? Perhaps not of the kind envisioned by the Puritans. Joy and laughter mingled freely with regrets and tears. Yes, there were tears. They came unexpectedly and won unstinting respect. We became brothers and we knew it. As we approach journey's end we also know that the thoughts we share become increasingly special. To the naked eye those concrete walls still seem intact. But not to worry, the inner eye of the poet sees other things.

The Best Thing

William King

I learned how it feels to be free.
I learned a lot about me.
I learned how every negative don't go unpunished.
I learned that great minds don't speak rubbish.
I learned to not depend on others
and to do it yourself.
I learned life isn't all about golf,
or women, or wealth.

Serving this time taught me a lot.
Now I'm mentally moving with the world
even though I'm in a standstill like a block.

But the best thing I learned
from all the above
is how to love.

My New Wife

Josue "Big Bear" Pierre

Lend me your ears,
you who come from far and near:
I've become your with-it
William Shakespeare.

When I didn't feel like much,
poetry became my crutch.
I grabbed up a pen and pad
and scribbled much.

Whoever knew there was so much
waiting there within my touch?
Not me! How could this be?

I talked to you and I found a way
—another way, is what I say—
to put my feelings on display
and douse my anger with word play.

Your love is as comforting as drugs
sent to me from up above.
I shoulda found you sooner,
instead of winding up a loser.

I cherish the day you came into my life,
damn, why couldn't you just be my wife?
I promise to love, and to stroke my pen
  deep within you.
Today I take my vow to you;
  always faithful, always true.

Your name is Poetry,
I've made you my wife.
You'll mother my kids
and lighten my life.

But quit on me with a backward wave
and we'll both wind up in an early grave.
For if you run and leave me ultra blue
I'll simply close the book on you.

Coming of Age

David Hutchings

Yeah, I get it. So let me share what went down. I was raised by my grandmother, a sober, loving woman. But my family were mostly addicts or dealers. I don't know if my mother was an addict but she was caught up in street life and drugs were a constant in her scene. Her brother, my uncle Jonah, was my hero. He was with the military overseas. He often sent me letters and gifts. My grandmother died when I was twelve years old, and I took it hard. Uncle Jonah flew over to help us grieve. But he merely upped the ante. My mother and I returned home from a happy back-to-school shopping trek, but as we stepped in the door our mood turned to horror. The house was trashed and all the valuables were gone—jewelry, television, stereo, my video games, and my bike—even the funeral money. I was staggered. I was crushed. I was angry. I was outraged. What kind of creep stole toys from a kid and money for his own mother's funeral? My hero, that's who. Uncle Jonah had robbed his family to feed his addiction. He also stole our fragile sense of safety, trashed my innocence, and ended my childhood. His single act destroyed our family. Mom and I fell out. Then, when I turned fifteen, she threw me out. I sold drugs to survive. I was too young to get my own apartment, so I went to live with my aunt and cousins. I'd heard my aunt was an addict but I never saw it till she came copping for a hit. I was already ashamed to be a dealer, now even more so. At first I wouldn't sell to her. I tried to act like I wasn't dealing. But she knew. Everyone knew. How can you tell an addict you don't have any drugs when you're living in their house? Yeah, I got a trick for you. Anytime I'd go to sleep they'd catch me for my stash and I'd have to pay that back. It got so bad I slept with my money and drugs in my underwear. It was crazy. I remember I told her wanted to go back to school. "School?!" she said: "Is you crazy? You better get out there and get that money, Nigga." So, my dealing was accepted and respected, both. I buy my own clothes, I pay for groceries, I pay the bills–I'm a *man*. Just a few years earlier, my aunts and uncles used to give me money for the holidays. "Here, go buy you something nice," they'd say. Now I'm only sixteen and they're begging me for money or drugs or credit. That's how I wound up with no one to stop me on my downward spiral. You said my writing showed my key issue; a "deep, knee-jerk hatred of authority." Really? Well, Fuck you, Professor! Just kidding. I looked back over my poems and stuff to see what I'd written. Hmm. I slept on it. I got to connect the dots and catch the pattern. Dot number one: my childhood hero taught me to despise anyone in a government suit. Dots number two through a thousand: if an officer or judge came into my orbit I fell into a trance and acted out a crazy dance, blowing bitter raspberries and pushing a scornful middle finger in the direction of a ghost, that uniformed Jonah from my past. Well, that was then and this is now. I'm wide awake this morning and old attitudes are fading. Like most of us here though, I'm trapped in the endgame of a childhood nightmare. I hope that's not my last word.

Last Words

William King

My last words will be memorable,
    maybe even remarkable.
When I leave this earth,
    they may well say that he died as he lived,
    and was a great man from birth.

I'll use my freedom to save lives and teach.
I'll stand at a podium and hold folks alert,
or peer from a pulpit and share sermons at church,
telling–and showing–how we all can
                                outrun pain and hurt.

Most of my old friends will say that I changed,
though some may resort to calling me names,
starting with shame, passing through lame,
                                        and ending with nerd;
but they'll never forget–my last words.

My Eulogy, Please

Josue "Big Bear" Pierre

From the womb to the tomb,
life's most bitter test,
can give birth to the best
and wean out the rest.

Talk the talk or walk the walk?
Never been an angel, I confess.
I used to be young and naive,
easy for a hoodlum to impress,
so I lost my wings in '99
and life became a mess.

Prison showed me books and wisdom
and whenever things went wrong
in some scenes I didn't belong
these taught me to be strong.

At last I'm seeing sense;
from the cradle to the grave
life is just a quest,
so before I'm laid to rest,
I pray you say I gave life
nothing but the best.

Have You Heard?

Joseph Birch

It's my own heart
that my crazy feelings tore:
Have you heard?
To boldly go
where no man's gone before:
Have you heard?
To grow up and become mature:
Have you heard?
To get real rehab
and your courage to restore:
Have you heard?
Passing through another door,
feet firmly on the floor.
Have you heard?
That's my last word.

Entertainment

Ron Godbold

Last words can be a column in a newspaper.
Last words can cause problems.
Last words can uplift.
Last words can bring a stream of tears.
Last words can be bright as the sun.
Last words can make a friend run.
So be careful what you say.
You never know when you might be
entertaining an angel.
That's my last word.

Turning Points

Rudy Bisnauth

My words can never be last,
so I've placed them first before the last,
but let me tellya, in this class
epiphanies hit me like windmill grass.

Don't just overcome the struggle,
but push hard, move on, and surpass.

I'll pass that along to the next class.

Wisdom and love.
Without them our hearts
shrink and die
in a steel glove.

Lead teams and take turns,
pursue what you dream of.

Don't fall in line
with the walking dead,
thank the guide
who dispelled the dread.

And here's my point of no return:
keep the hopes up and the lights on
so that when the gates open
we know which way to turn.

Lasting Words

Moises Colon

I learned that just like the rest of us, once they're released, words have their own lives. I see that words can be weighty or light, heavy or gentle, upsetting or soothing. They can inspire or depress, build or destroy. They can win you a vote, lose you a job, or show who you really are. So be careful of first words, and in-between words—and especially last words. If they ring true they can live on forever in people's hearts and minds.

A Rising Son

Sheldon Arnold

Gone is the fun,
through the darkness I run
at the speed of sound
like the blast of a gun.

The battle was fought
and they thought they won
by throwing me down
like a burning bun.

But I caught the light of a rising sun
and I now too am surely one—
so I'll have the last word
when all's said and done.

Tribute

William King

With no family near, I grew up here, in clink.
I learned through you, to be a man and to think.
These moments with my peers
taught more than all life's years.

You guys opened my eyes; I saw indeed
there's more to life than sex and weed.
You're my heroes believe it or not,
and I'm not just saying that 'cos you're all I got.

Moe taught us to prize our families;
Dre warned of corruption and greed;
Pitt's inner depth made my mind bleed;
Ron's a great freestyle as we all can see;
Arnold opened my eyes to Black history;
Birch showed me a leader, strong and true;
Bear's a great raconteur, poems and all,
Neville's always got my back
making sure I never fall.
Richard showcased age and wisdom,
and what John gave is plain to see:
to stand right up
and share our truth
when we get free.

The Rock

Richard Moore

So, what is remorse? It's a stepping-stone to growth–
real growth, honest to goodness, once and forever
change. I call remorse my rock. Let me tell you how
I came to find it. And how you might, too. First,
remorse only comes after a "wrong *doing*." I had
to realize that my doings–my *actions*–truly were
wrong. After I accepted that I also began to see that
my actions had harmed countless people. That I
was a negative, hurtful influence, and an especially
rotten example for kids. That rock of mine, remorse,
inspired me to take a truly deep and truly honest
look into myself. That was when I came to realize
that up until that moment I'd been blind to all the
harm I'd caused. Since then I've seen with wide
open eyes that truly remorseful ex-offenders like
me *show* our remorse. Real remorse is more than a
feeling, more than guilt and shame. It's more than
a phrase, too. Saying "I'm sorry"is a good start but
not nearly enough. If we're truly remorseful we *act*. I
don't mean just looking backwards and shaking our
heads in wonderment that we were the benumbed
zombie who did all those terrible things. Yes, we *will*
look back and shake our heads. But when I say that a
remorseful person *acts*, what I really mean is making
good and giving back. We help others. We set about
renewing our communities. We become productive,
law-abiding citizens. We *show* our children *right
doings*. We make sure they get a decent education. We
set them onto right roads. If you talk but don't act,
remorse is just a word.

Hope Chest

Andre Rivera

God puts the strong
to the toughest tasks,
and now, at the end
of this eye-opening class,
I break free from old thinking
and ditch my mask,
thanking God almighty
that I'm free at last.

And so good friends
in this community chest,
let's rebuild our lives
on righteousness;
where it goes or ends
we can only guess;
we live for today
at peace with the next;
for what we now have,
we say thanks,
–you taught us success;
for what we don't have,
we're unstressed;
every day we wake,
we know we're blessed.

Farewell

Herburtho Benjamin

Farewell and fair well,
sounds the liberty bell.

Hearts assail
the justice scale,
but souls, my friend,
are not for sale.

This ark is made to sail;
if you think you're gonna fail
come follow me, and we'll prevail.

Farewell and fair well,
sounds the liberty bell.

14. A Whole New Life

If I'm the creator of all my strife
I can also fashion a whole new life
–Chandler Haste

From each crime are born bullets
that will one day seek out in you
where the heart lies.
–Pablo Neruda

Come join our happy band of brothers. Pull up a steel and fiberglass chair within our concrete box cell. Ignore the barred window behind you that overlooks those glistening rolls of razor wire. This is our last session. I'm hoping the takeaway will be the overall message of the past three months. The poems were a means to an end. They supplemented a set of life-changing discussion readings that I've compiled over the years. The whole thing–what German psychologists of the Berlin School call the *Gestalt*–is a different way of thinking about life and its problems. That's what I'm hoping to deliver. So here we go, then. Let me attempt to clarify, as promised, precisely what it takes to survive a bullet to the heart.

How to Survive a Bullet to the Heart

John Wareham

What a time we've had! If you glance back over your poems, you'll see they're milestones on a journey to enlightenment.

Enlightenment! Is that a fuzzy idea, or what?

Taoists say that to be enlightened is to be in harmony with the universe. Christians say it's about being reborn and putting away childish things. My own take is that it's all about waking up and getting real.

Too many people sleepwalk through life. They think they're making their own choices but they're not. Psychologists call that the Illusion of Autonomy.

From childhood onwards, these sleepwalkers bumble through life mindlessly reacting to their upbringings and environment.

They obey and do whatever they're told. Or they engage in negative obedience and mindlessly do the opposite of whatever they're told. Either way, life proves desperately unfulfilling—and, all too often, dangerous.

You've been told that you're here because you made a wrong choice and committed a crime. But, legally, if there was no intention to commit a crime, then there was no crime at all. Defending himself of murder, Shakespeare's character, Hamlet, the Prince of Denmark, makes the point:

If Hamlet when he's not himself does wrong,
then Hamlet does it not.
Who does it then? His madness.
If it be so, Hamlet is of the faction that is wronged;
His madness is poor Hamlet's enemy.

So Hamlet blames his madness for doing wrong. What Hamlet calls madness, I call mindlessness—the absence of authentic contemplation and truly rational choice.

I hope you weren't offended when I said in our first class that your judgment of why you committed your crime was most likely hopelessly flawed; that while your reasoning *seemed* okay it actually obscured infinitely deeper issues. You were, literally, ignorant of the forces in play. So no matter what you *thought* was happening, you were *wronged*—you, too, were a victim.

Sure, you *thought* you intended to commit a crime. You *thought* you committed that crime because you believed you could get away with it. You *imagined*, and other people told you, forcefully, I'm sure, that you could've—and should've—made other choices. In fact, your upbringing and environment denied you any other option. *You could conceive of no other choice—and so, for you, none existed.*

It was as if, in the course of growing up, an invisible net had been thrown over you. You could see what others were doing, but you were unaware of the net that defined—and confined—your own behavior. Your life became a terrible struggle and you never truly knew why.

Frustrated and angered by your own powerlessness, you committed a crime. At the time you didn't understand that victims abide at both ends of a gun. Your weapon may have been a revolver, a knife, a fist, a boot, or a car. It may have been the nod of your head, or the down-turning of your thumb. It may even have been silence in the presence of potential violence or death. Whatever the weapon, it had been a long time in the making, and was formed by the same people and forces that created that net—that trap.

Bad things happen to most of us growing up. Hamlet called them "the slings and arrows of outrageous fortune, the whips and scorns of time." Let's be honest, those slings, arrows, whips, and scorns were worse for you guys than for most. That's just a fact. One way or another, your norm was poverty, poor parenting, verbal and physical and/or sexual abuse, inferior education, and racism. Whether you realized it or not, anxiety, frustration, resentment, and anger built up within you. Feelings of worthlessness and depression followed.

These sentiments evolved into at least a couple of core beliefs. First, *it is impossible for me to meet my survival needs and live a dignified life within the system*. Second, *it will therefore be okay for me to get what I need by any means necessary*.

An unhappy transformation inescapably followed. You became a robot or a renegade. You took drugs or dealt drugs. If you took them you anesthetized your troubled heart, but you remained a child hoping that others would take care of you. If you sold drugs you became independent, you became a *man*—or so you thought.

But any satisfaction was short-lived. Both strategies were self-defeating. The immediate problem momentarily went away, but your *situation* got worse. Taking drugs turned you into a junkie, dealing them made you a criminal.

Now, just to stay in place you needed more drugs or more criminal acts, or both.

Unless you were an out-and-out sociopath—a person without empathy, a liar without a conscience or a heart—you suffered increasing guilt.

At the time, you were probably so numbed that you didn't realize what was happening.

Unconsciously though, deep down inside, you wanted to draw attention to your plight. You also wanted this life you imagined you had chosen to end. You wanted to be punished and thereby expiate your terrible guilt. And, you know what? Your unconscious found a way to make that happen.

So let's make couple of things crystal clear.

If firing a weapon caused you to wind up inside these walls, then you are a victim. Becoming a victim was outside your control.

It was something that happened *to* you. That is an *explanation*. That is the truth. It is not a lie. It is not a mere excuse.

If you see it clearly, if you truly get–and accept–this big idea, a new world will open. Not only are you off the hook, *now you will be able to make a conscious, rational choice never to be a victim again.*

If you return to jail, however, the explanation will no longer be valid. From this point forward, any new offense will represent a conscious choice. Any words offered in defense of your crime will be an excuse, not an explanation.

So, the apparent free pass for any and all of your past misdeeds actually came with a price tag. Enlightenment always does. On the bright side, to redeem that debt you only need to live a happy, productive life.

So let's think about the way forward.

Specifically, let's think about USA, Liberty, and SAM.

USA

No matter what happened to you along the way, and no matter your crime, the *self* at the center of your being is perfect. It is the calm center in the eye of the storm. No matter the hurricane about you, the center remains calm.

As children, we know this in our hearts. But adults tell us differently and we come to doubt our value. We bow to the pressure of other people's opinions–loved ones and enemies, both–and accept that we are flawed and unworthy. But as, Dr. Albert Ellis–judged by his peers as the most helpful psychoanalyst of the twentieth century–observed, "If intrinsic value exists at all, you get it because you define it, you choose it, you decide to have it. You are 'good' or 'deserving' because you think so, not because anyone else awards you this kind of inherent value."

Like the eagle, you are the product of millions of years of evolution. That king of the birds never doubts itself. It merely focuses on its needs. Does the sparrow consider itself less worthy than the eagle? I don't think so.

Worthy is just an opinion. There's no need to rate our *selves* at all. We are as worthy of being on the planet as any other creature. To acknowledge this fact is the first step to creating *unconditional self-acceptance*—USA.

When you have USA—and you can make a gift of it to yourself right now—you value yourself merely because you are alive and kicking. For that reason alone you "deserve" an enjoyable life.

Now you lose the overweening need for others' approval. As long as you crave that, you're unconsciously hoping that praise, admiration, and acceptance—from colleagues and employers as well as friends and family—will heal wounds inflicted during childhood.

Sure, acceptance may confer some practical advantages in the here and now. But that still has nothing to do with your actual human worth.

To stop this kind of self-defeating defining is to kill the craving for outside approval. It is also to end the crazy habit of rating your own worthiness, of getting down on your *self* for imagined defects.

Oh, happy day!

Now is the time to gratefully receive your gift of unconditional self-acceptance, and shift your focus to your thoughts, words, and actions.

Liberty

To embrace liberty is to switch liberating beliefs for imprisoning beliefs.

We already considered a couple of imprisoning beliefs: *I can't get what I need within the system—so it is okay to get what I want by any means necessary.*

Here's a sad fact: when you were growing up these beliefs

made sense. Back then you had to fend for yourself in a world you were ill equipped to handle. But that was then. People cut you slack and let you get away with stuff. Then one day the music stopped. The world had changed, but you hadn't noticed. Now you were no longer a child. Now you got held accountable for your actions. These old imprisoning beliefs became exactly that. You wound up in jail.

Now–right here this very moment–is the time to align your beliefs with the way today's world works. Now is the time to get real.

American pop philosopher Will Rogers said, "It ain't the things we know that gets us into trouble, it's the things we know that just ain't so."

Only when we realize–and accept–that a belief is false can we get it out of the brain.

Trouble is, *the imprisoning beliefs we need to scrap are often those we cherish.* We need them to justify our prejudices and failures.

Worse yet, come what may, because of the way the mind works, we will fight–literally–to hold on to our imprisoning beliefs rather than give them up. We delude ourselves that we're in some kind of heaven and battle for the right to remain incarcerated!

Wishful thinking becomes the norm. Bad luck becomes a constant companion.

Imprisoning beliefs are also self-fulfilling. If we believe that something can't be done, then failure follows. *I can't get there from here,* is a neat example of an imprisoning belief. A liberating belief would be, *If I come up with a plan, hone my skills, and persevere, then I can get whatever I realistically need.*

The trick in life is to become a realistic optimist.

Identifying and acknowledging previously unrecognized behavior patterns triggers a change of consciousness–enlightenment!

Our eyes open. Now we see that we were not making rational, conscious choices. Now we're compelled to acknowledge the existence of another level of consciousness. Like it or not, we are pushed into a new kind of existence.

SAM

Buddha said that the wise man should make of himself an island that no flood may overcome. The way to make that happen is to replace self-defeating behaviors with *self-affirming maneuvers*—SAM.

That means *actively* pursuing your own best interests. It means consciously setting long term goals, then setting milestones and *going for them*—one step at time, slowly but surely, steadily and relentlessly.

For openers, such maneuvers should focus on acquiring, honing, and selling a marketable skill.

That skill should enable you to earn *sufficient income* to survive, and then go on to build a satisfying, dignified life. It should have *special meaning* for you; becoming a counselor and helping young people avoid your mistakes might be one way to do that. It should also be something at which you can become the *best in the world*.

If that "best in the world" idea sounds daunting, it needn't. Becoming the best in *your* world is just a matter of creating a narrow niche for yourself in your own backyard. Your aim is to become the neighborhood go-to guy—the fellow known to have the valuable skill needed to solve a tricky problem.

Self-affirming maneuvers naturally include showing up on time, going the extra mile, and doing what everyone agrees is a first-rate job. Add to that list, working on your people skills, smiling, sharing kind words, helping others, and, most crucially, taking care of yourself—attending the gym not the tobacconist, that kind of thing.

I bet you know all this, already. So let me be blunt and share something we also know but don't like to talk about.

Sometimes things go awry and we lose the plot.

Well, *that* is the precisely the moment for yet another self-affirming maneuver.

That is exactly the time to consciously select an uplifting, liberating thought, then follow through with a daring leap of faith. When we do that, we stir the unconscious. Intuition gradually takes over and illumines the way forward.

As you know, I'm a convert of the Jedis. We tap into the benediction of our *Star Wars* seer and sage, Obi-Wan Kenobi. "May the force be with you," he likes to whisper. Maybe you'd like to become a Jedi, too. There are no initiations, no fees, no priests or potentates, no dogmas, no smells and no bells. You only have to believe in the force and share our salutation, "May the force be with you." How hard is that? We're not starry-eyed, by the way. We only believe in the force because we've discovered that when we're tapped into it we feel great and everything goes smoothly. And if we fall off the force, things go wrong and we feel bad. That's when we call for SAM.

If the goal of life is to comfort each other and leave a meaningful legacy, then within these walls might be the best place on earth to practice some self-affirming maneuvers. The walking wounded are all around. You see them clearly, right, that courtyard full of feisty young blind men? You know that their vision's awry, and that their macho fronting is just a mask for suffering and trepidation. *Your* self-affirming maneuver can change *their* lives, too.

Your smile can bring out the sun.

Your kind word can ease a deep pain.

Your friendly gesture can dislodge a bullet and set a heart to healing.

May the force be with you.

THE POETS AND WRITERS

Sheldon Arnold, 29, was formerly a music producer. He was convicted of robbery and burglary, and has fifteen years of a sixteen-year sentence left to serve. Mr. Arnold's interests include music, politics, religion, literature, and quantum physics. He is unsure of his plans upon release.

Herburtho Benjamin, 30, formerly a mason tender, was convicted of voluntary manslaughter. He was sentenced to twenty years, and has fifteen left to serve. His interests include construction, fishing, filming, sailing, botany, and collecting art. His goal upon release is to become realistic and self-reliant, and to share love.

Joseph Birch, 48, characterizes himself as a recovering neophyte. He was convicted of possession of an illegal firearm and sentenced to twelve years to life, of which he has seven to serve. He notes that "I was expected to become somebody to respect in the community, and I'm hoping I can still achieve that by becoming a youth counselor when I get released."

Rudy Bisnauth, 28, formerly a college student, was convicted of second degree murder and sentenced to twenty-five years to life. His conviction is currently on appeal. His interests include "completing as many educational courses as possible while incarcerated, then becoming free, providing for my family, making the most of my life and becoming someone to look up to." Upon release he intends to continue his education and become an entrepreneur.

Moises Colon, 45, was convicted of possession of drugs, conspiracy, criminal possession of a weapon, and criminal impersonation. He was sentenced to serve twelve to twenty-five years, and currently has seven to serve. His interests include law, business, reading, and technology. Upon release he intends to become self-employed in real estate, or own a franchise.

Ron Godbold, 45, was convicted of criminal possession of a controlled substance and sentenced to ten years. His interests include freestyle poetry. Upon release he wants to follow Christian teachings, and help inner city youth.

David Hutchings, 42, was expected to become an architect or an actor. He was convicted of robbery and sentenced to serve thirty-two years, of which twenty-one remain on his sentence. His interests include music, fashion and film. Upon release "I intend to become a decent guy, help others, and stay out of jail."

Kenneth Johnson, a cat burglar and holdup man, had a jailhouse conversion at age forty-two, after reading Jean-Paul Sartre in John Wareham's first Rikers Island class. Mr. Johnson subsequently returned to Rikers to share the Eagles message that life and destiny are created by everyday decisions. A smooth, street-smart character with the smoky manners of a jazz musician, he performed his spoken-word verse at poetry cafes, and, notably, on the steps of the Albany Statehouse, protesting the Rockefeller drug laws. He died of a heart attack in 2003, at age forty-nine.

Andre Jones, 46, formerly a construction worker, was convicted of manslaughter. He was sentenced to seventeen years of incarceration and has eight left to serve. His interests include studying law and reading. Upon release he intends to become a paralegal.

William King, 33, was expected to become an actor or comedian. Instead he gravitated to roles as disc jockey, dog trainer, public speaker, and pimp. He was convicted of second degree murder and first degree robbery. He has six years left on an eighteen-year sentence. Upon release, "I'd like to lead a normal life as a good citizen, work as a volunteer, and spend time with my kids."

Richard Moore, 49, was expected to become a doctor or an actor, but instead qualified as an American Sign Language Interpreter. He was convicted of drug sales and was sentenced to thirty-one years, of which he has five months to serve. Upon release he intends to "go back to college, help other people, and open a restaurant."

Josue "Big Bear" Pierre, 36, formerly a chemical machine worker, was convicted of drug trafficking. He was sentenced to serve nine years. He had sixteen months left to serve when released on the day of graduating the 2013 Eagles class. His interests are poetry and creative writing. He hopes to become a mystery writer.

Andre Rivera, 34, formerly a retail store assistant manager, was convicted of gun possession. He was sentenced to eleven years and five years post release. He currently has three years left to serve. Upon release he intends to finish college courses, and seek a job in the music industry.

Neville Wells, 52, was formerly a club manager and concert promoter. Following a car fatality while driving under the influence, he was convicted of vehicular homicide, a second degree murder offense, and sentenced to serve seventeen years to life. He currently has seven years left to serve on that sentence. His interests include drug counseling, athletics, literature, and the arts. He applies his organizational talents to delivering prison rehabilitation programs, and recruits and mentors inmates who attend the Downstate Eagles program. Upon release he intends to "find a job where I can apply all that I have learned in prison to serve my community, and make a real difference in the lives of others, especially those who fall from grace, as I did."

The worth of that is that which it contains,
and that is this, and this with thee remains.
–William Shakespeare

Index of Poets and Writers

HOW TO BREAK OUT OF PRISON—THE JOHN WAREHAM LIFE-CHANGER

Unlock the Mind and go free now

"All prisons are mental prisons; they lock from the inside and you own the key, so only you can let yourself out."

–John Wareham

"**Invigorating**—bold ideas and an almost cocky tone combine with charm and edgy intricate logic to create a book that will result in a fresh and energized perspective."

—Library Journal

"**Powerful . . .** Wareham's unusual premise, readable real-life examples, and self-assessment personality quizzes will appeal to those seeking to change their lives."

—Publishers Weekly

"**Astonishing** . . . showcases Wareham's gift for unlocking the mind and showing us how to live the life of our deepest dreams."

—Kevin Roberts,
Chief Executive, Saatchi & Saatchi

"**A moving, life-altering work,** uniquely honed in the disparate corridors of money and power, hope, and despair."

—Howard Frank, Ph.D.,
Dean, Maryland Business School

Welcome Rain Publishers, LLC

New York

THE PRESIDENT'S THERAPIST—THE PSYCHO-POLITICAL THRILLER THAT APPLIES THE WAREHAM LIFE CHANGING TECHNIQUES

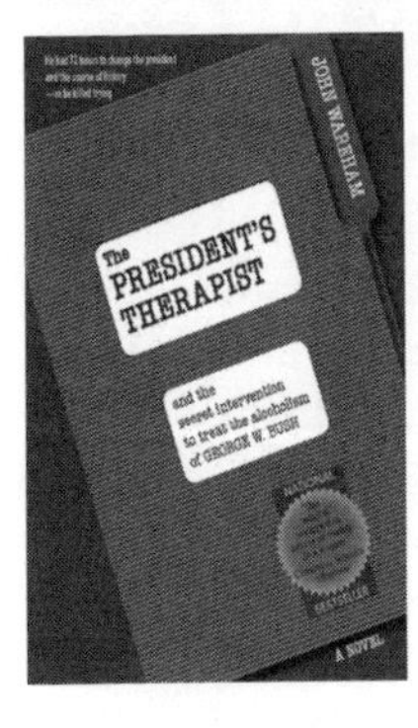

He had seventy-two hours to change the president and the course of history —or be killed trying.

Insurgents within the White House retain a uniquely gifted psychologist to help President George W. Bush address a clandestine addiction to alcohol and reverse the course of the Iraq War. The assignment meets with astonishing success—until foul forces come into play.

"A winner—a 'what-if' novel wrapped in layers of reality that offers an unnerving 'case study' of alcoholism in the White House. We enter a series of psychological and forensic intelligence forays engendered by the U.S. secret service along with a certain Dr. Mark Alter, leadership psychologist and wizard at 'coaching' CEO's into restoring their acumen and performance. In this case, however, the patient is none other than President George W. Bush."

—Christian Science Monitor

"A literary and political masterpiece." **—Malachy McCourt,** Green Party candidate for governor of New York State

"Unique, highly recommended, and sure to please . . .
Told from the perspective of the president's psychologist, this is a story with a unique twist and perspective."

—Midwest Reviews

Welcome Rain Publishers, LLC

New York

CHANCEY ON TOP—WAREHAM'S WISDOM WITHIN A LOVE TRIANGLE

The price of ambition, the value of love, and the meaning of dreams

Just as his big-time dreams seem about to come true, Chandler Haste glances into the rear view mirror of the limousine bearing him across New York's Triboro Bridge, and catches the reflection of a scorching affair from his past overleaping oceans to engulf him.

"Dazzling . . . a delicious literary bonbon . . . —*New York Observer* **"Inspired . . .** philosophically savvy, **hilarious,** whimsical." — *Kirkus Reviews* **"Stunning . . .** an ardent . . . an affecting . . . assured exploration of moral quandaries."—*Publishers Weekly* **"Poetic gold!** The finest contemporary showcasing of the sonnet form." —Charles DeFanti, professor of literature, and author of *The Wages of Expectation; A Biography of Edward Dahlberg.* **"Shattering . . .** Those who find their wisdom in **wild and witty** packaging will love *Chancey* . . . **deeply moving."** —Bernard Berkowitz, Ph.D., author of *How to Be Your Own Best Friend* **"Magnificent . . . racy and contentious** . . . literary and erudite . . . **profound and moving.** Captures the inner conflicts of conscience and provides **authentic insights** into the struggles of upward strivers." —Harry Levinson, clinical psychologist, Harvard Medical School

Welcome Rain Publishers, LLC

New York

SONNETS FOR SINNERS
EVERYTHING ONE NEEDS TO KNOW ABOUT ILLICIT LOVE
by John Wareham

America's Sweetheart

#1 Bestselling Sonnet Anthology upon Valentine's Day release.

"JUST IN TIME FOR VALENTINE'S DAY, John Wareham found poetry in the lines and lies of world-class cheaters, like Tiger Woods, former senator John Edwards and Prince Charles, and in laments of spurned spouses like Elizabeth Edwards and Princess Diana."–*New York Daily News* **"Deliciously tempting** . . . filled with passion, desire and carnal lust. . . famous and contemporary love triangles seen from all sides."–*Ambush Magazine* **"A passionate lure** to the sonnet's delights." –David Stanford Burr, Professor of Poetry, New York University, Barnes & Noble anthologist **"Happily destined, like Milton's Paradise Lost,** to find its readers." –Don Foster, Professor of Literature, Vassar College.

Welcome Rain Publishers, LLC

Corner of a Foreign Field

Illustrated Poetry of Brilliant Unsung Poets

Crisp, contemporary *Daily Mail* photographs of World War I battlefields, battles, and heartbreaking homefront scenes complement poems written during the war, many by eminent writers, but most, by brilliant unsung poets.

Muhammad Ali
The Illustrated Biography
by Christine Kidney

Throughout his extraordinary career, Muhammad Ali's influence on boxing changed the sport forever. This book charts the life of this fascinating and complex man from the time he caught the public eye when, as Cassius Clay, he won a Gold Medal at the Olympic Games in Rome.

Christine Kidney is a writer and editor and lives in Gloucestershire, England, with her family. Her most recently published work is a pictorial biography of Audrey Hepburn.

Who Would I Be If My Father Had Been Someone Else?

This startling and beautiful book is a valiant attempt to answer this universal and searching question by mining the recollections of forty sons and daughters from every imaginable background. The forty portraits are limited to two 350-word paragraphs of each subject's own words. The recollection of each father, accompanied by an archival photograph, is paired with a moving evaluation of the son's or daughter's heritage, and illustrated by a contemporary portrait. The result of a lifetime's research, this book is unlike any other study published.

Jess Maghan recently retired as professor of criminal justice at the University of Illinois at Chicago. *Sam Lindberg* has had a long career as a professional photographer, having collaborated with Irving Penn and other distinguished artists.

The Artist's Wife, *Max Phillips.*

"Alma Mahler Gropius, the 'wild brat' of fin de siècle Vienna, is the graceless subject of Phillips's (Snakebite Sonnet) bitingly sarcastic historical novel. Alma's forthright narration succeeds in conveying the personality of a complex, indomitable woman who behaved 'more like a man than a woman,' fascinated Vienna's art world and, later, Hollywood's expatriate colony, and who lived life exactly as she wished, bravely and without hypocrisy." —*Publishers Weekly*

Welcome Rain Publishers, LLC

New York